The Lost Art and Science of Professional Wrestling

David "Shriek" Chapman

*Author, Owner, Promoter, Booker,
Wrestler, Manager, Referee, Heel*

To Jeremy,
My Wrestling Hero

2

FORWARD

I always find the stories of how someone became a professional wrestling fan to be quite fascinating and, in my case, it may help shed some light on everything that you are about to read in this book. I was a young boy who every weekend would go to my grandparents for breakfast with the family and after breakfast was over, I would run off into my aunt's room as she had a TV in her room and it was private. I was around 12 years old or so and I was flipping around the channels looking for cartoons but instead, I stumbled upon a squared circle perfectly framed in the middle of my screen that then cut to someone on the microphone announcing someone when upbeat music suddenly played, people started screaming and the cameras cut to what I later found out was Hulk Hogan walking down to the ring playing to the crowd. This was the largest human being I had ever seen and I was instantly mesmerized. On top of that, the lights, the color, the excitement, and most of all, the emotion was unlike anything I had ever seen before. They then announced his opponent as the Iron Sheik. People clearly didn't like him and he was wearing a rather large belt around his waist (which they made clear later was the world champion's belt) but I really didn't know much more as I didn't have any idea what was going on and it honestly didn't matter. I was glued to the screen and five minutes and 40 seconds later when Hulk Hogan pinned the Iron Sheik and won that world championship belt, I was so wrapped up in it that I was screaming my head off just like everyone at that event even though again, I honestly didn't know what the rules were or even why the pin mattered. The show ended and I was hooked but things took a rather interesting turn the very next week.

That week's breakfast was an eternal affair as I desperately wanted to return to that glorious wrestling product that I had seen. Breakfast of course ended, I rushed to my aunt's room and began flipping the channels trying to find that wrestling show. As soon as I saw two men rolling around in the ring I stopped searching and dug in. What I didn't realize until later was that there were two wrestling shows on TV at that time on different stations and I had inadvertently turned to the other one. This show was a little different as it wasn't nearly as colorful as last week and I didn't recognize anyone. I really didn't care and when the announcer said that after the commercial break there would be a world heavyweight title match, I got really excited figuring I was either going to see that match with Hulk Hogan again or possibly a new match with him. Imagine my surprise when after the commercial break I saw a ring surrounded by a steel cage and the announcer, who again I didn't recognize, announce that the challenger was coming to the ring and his name was Ric Flair. I was confused of course but as soon as Also Sprach Zarathustra (Ric's theme music) kicked into gear and the man made his entrance, there was no way I was changing that channel. Ric was mesmerizing. It wasn't nearly as larger-than-life and energetic as Hulk Hogan from last week but the flowing robes, the grace, the confidence, and intensity - it was stunning. They then announced his opponent - the world champion. Again, I was surprised as I thought this was Hulk Hogan but instead, it was a guy that didn't look much different than any person I saw on the street or even in my own family named Harley Race and his entrance was quite matter-of-fact as well (a far cry from last week). It didn't really matter as I was enthralled and curious how this was going to play out and what the ring being surrounded by a steel cage was going to have to do with it. 33 minutes and 29 seconds later I sat, jaw on the ground, stunned, and simply said to myself "now THAT is a world heavyweight champion, I have no idea what that clown last week won". These two guys beat the holy hell out of each other. Ric flair was a bloody mess. Harley Race may not look like it but he was tough as nails. This was a fight and it was a fight over who deserved to own that championship belt. It absolutely blew my mind and set me down a very particular path in professional wrestling and more important, professional wrestling philosophy.

It was only later that I found out that one station was showing the WWF and the other station was showing the NWA and it just so happened that it was sweeps week so they both were pulling out their best shot to pull in viewers despite these two matches occurring almost a year apart. This served as a valuable lesson, and coincidentally a great launching point for this book, as to the true power and variety in professional wrestling. I had many opportunities in my youth to see both shows and I always gravitated to the far superiorly booked NWA. Some people will say that since the WWF (now WWE) ended up being the promotion that lasted it was the superior product and more indicative of what people wanted to see. They cannot be more wrong as the moment the WWF/E became a global powerhouse was the attitude era when they finally adopted the booking philosophies that will be illustrated in this book while at the same time the NWA (which had morphed into WCW by then) abandoned those booking philosophies destroying the company from the inside.

Drawing on a lifetime of the love of wrestling and deep dives into the booking styles and decisions of the Masters I was able to hone, refine and expand my booking knowledge to create a successful product in my own promotions. This book, while it can never be a complete repository of that knowledge, will serve as a guideline, a framework, a reference book, or whatever you want to call it to help those who wish to have a firmer grasp on the psychological power that professional wrestling, when executed properly, is capable of. It doesn't matter if you're a fan, a wrestler, a promoter, a valet, a manager, cameraman, ring crew, announcer, or any other person involved in the wonderful world of professional wrestling you can benefit by, and gain a greater understanding of, not necessarily what is going on, but of what is truly possible, inside the squared circle (and of course outside as well). With that thought in mind, I invite you to explore the lost art and science of professional wrestling.

TABLE OF CONTENTS

1. Kayfabe is not dead – even though you think it is.
2. Three rules in the ring – and only three.
3. Know your role – we're all in this together.
4. Psychology in wrestling – the male soap opera.
5. Training mechanics – you're not being taught correctly...or at all.
6. Character development – you on steroids (metaphorically).
7. Physical development – you on steroids (literally).
8. Structuring a match – by not planning out every move.
9. How to book a story – just ask one question.
10. The crowd – what they want and stop ignoring them.
11. How to bleed – and when and why.
12. Match Types
    1. Battle Royal
    2. NO DQ
    3. Steel Cage
    4. Texas death match
    5. First blood match
    6. Belt suspended from the ring
    7. Face gets 5 minutes with the heel manager
    8. Ladder Match
13. Hardcore wrestling – you actually do need skills.
14. Backyard/Modern wrestling – learn to slow down.
15. Conclusion – where do we go from here

KAYFABE IS NOT DEAD
(even though you think it is)

5

Nearly every wrestler and wrestling fan that I meet will proudly proclaim to anyone who cares to listen that kayfabe is dead which causes me to roll my eyes and embark a bit of a journey where I show them that kayfabe is alive and well and still very much utilized by those at the top of their game.

If you know what the word "kayfabe" means go ahead and skip this paragraph but for those that don't, some background information is in order. The definition of the word is not exactly concrete or easy to explain. In broad terms, it was used to refer to the fact that there was a desire to present professional wrestling as a legitimate contest as opposed to a staged presentation with predetermined outcomes. One manifestation of this would be that in order to maintain "kayfabe" certain things would or would not be allowed. For example, in the early to mid-1900s as heel and face wrestlers were traveling around the country there was a rather strict rule that they could not be seen traveling together. Furthermore, they could not be seen hanging out socially outside of a professional wrestling show nor entering or leaving the building together. All of this was done in order to maintain the illusion that this was a legitimate contest and that they legitimately did not like each other. Promoters at the time were so successful in maintaining this illusion that wrestling shows were often covered in the sports section of newspapers no different than boxing matches. The word "kayfabe" can also be used on occasion as a codeword from one worker in the business to another to suggest that something is being said or done that could be picked up by someone not in the know thus destroying the illusion. A very simple example of this would be two wrestlers discussing the finish to a match as a fan walks by and one simply says to the other "kayfabe" and the conversation immediately stops or pivots to a different topic. The fact that some members of the audience have known almost since the dawn of professional wrestling that it was scripted or that the outcomes were predetermined does not alter the fact that there was a concerted effort to maintain kayfabe in the wrestling business until the late 1900s.

There were two major events, or to be more accurate one major event and one evolving technology, that caused many people to believe that kayfabe was in fact dead. This is of course not accurate as I will demonstrate but first let's get a better understanding of what transpired to make people think this. There are a few incidents leading up to the first major event whereby kayfabe was broken and exposed to the public and perhaps the most famous one being where a wrestler named Hacksaw Jim Duggan and a wrestler named the Iron Sheik - heel and face rivals at the time - were caught drunk and doing drugs in a car together by police. There were a handful of other incidences similar to this and these individual incidents certainly didn't help matters but it was ultimately a single breaking of kayfabe that set up the first major blow to the idea as a whole. Before I get into that, however, a quick history lesson for those not in the know - prior to the single domination of the World Wrestling Entertainment (WWE) Company in 2022 when this book was originally written, there were territorial wrestling organizations whereby wrestlers were able to freely move around the country and wrestle for different organizations. Each organization was in charge of a territory that encompassed several states and each of these states would or would not have an athletic commission. States that did have athletic commissions often times had oversight over professional wrestling contests including regulations regarding medical status for licensing but far more importantly - the collection of taxes. Once Vince McMahon, the head of the WWE, had pretty much consolidated almost all of these territories under the WWE umbrella he was not happy that he was having to pay taxes in certain states on his shows, specifically New Jersey, and not others. McMahon knew there was a very simple way to get out of having to pay these taxes and in 1989 he decided to pull the trigger by testifying in front of the New Jersey State Senate that professional wrestling was in fact a staged competition and not a competitive sport and as such, not subject to oversight and taxation by the New Jersey State Athletic Commission. The headlines of almost every major newspaper and news show the next day was basically that Vince had admitted wrestling was "fake". I have no doubt this was a shocker for the remaining people who had placed a large amount of stock in wrestling being a legitimate competitive sport but for the rest of us it was no surprise and considering that professional wrestling would reach its highest level of fame and profitability in the years to come after this proves that it was not the deathblow that many people thought it would be.

The evolving technology that further did damage to kayfabe was the rise in the popularity of the internet. For almost 100 years professional wrestling relied on the fact that events taking place in one part of the country would rarely if ever, be reported or even known on the other side of the country. You could literally have a wrestler be a heel in California and six months later be a face in Florida with almost no one knowing. The interconnectivity of the Internet changed all that instantly. Due to the internet connectivity, match results that took place in one part of the country were instantly disseminated not only around the rest of the country but around the world with one click of a button. Further complicating things, a random encounter at a grocery store with a supposedly mute wrestler such as George "The Animal" Steel suddenly became passed around as a story about what a nice sweet, and intelligent conversationalist he truly is. The dreaded term "Smart Mark" also came about at this point in time and was used to refer to marks who were not only smart to the fact that wrestling was pre-determined but also the basic mechanics of what was going on inside the ring move-wise despite the fact that they lack any training whatsoever. The Internet being the cesspool of humanity that it is these smart marks were not merely content to let people know that they knew what was going on. In fact, they often times made a point of ruining things for other people or going out of the way to act contrary to the established rules of kayfabe. For example, it was extremely common at this time to find a group of smart marks in a crowd at a wrestling show booing the good guys and cheering on the bad guys for their own benefit and no one else's. While these people were incredibly annoying, they still presented a challenge to kayfabe as they not only knew it was staged but went out of their way to make sure everyone else focused on that as well. All these things combined - and many, many more - was the straw that broke the camel's back and made almost everyone at that time, and to this day, declare that Kayfabe was dead.

At this point, you have to be asking yourself "Why then Sir do you think Kayfabe is not dead"? In order to understand the answer to this question, you must first understand and appreciate the entire foundation that professional wrestling is built on – psychology. Yes, you read that correctly I said psychology and not amateur wrestler. The interviews, segments, moves, holds, counter moves, and counter holds are merely a method of expressing psychology and, as will be pointed out later, those things without psychology are useless. To understand how kayfabe relates to psychology you must first understand the concept of willing suspension of disbelief (if you aren't already aware of it). The willing suspension of disbelief is mostly associated with other forms of entertainment such as movies and TV shows and there is a striking number of parallels between these forms of entertainment and professional wrestling so let's start with a clear definition of willing suspension of disbelief. Simply put, the audience knows that what it is experiencing is a fabricated presentation and not fact but is willing to convince themselves or "pretend" that it is real in order to further enjoy the experience. For the most part, people don't go to the movies and then walk out and say "oh that was so fake those are just two actors those people aren't really in love" or "oh things don't blow up like that in space" or "that guy would've died if a bomb had gone off that close to him". Instead, the audience is willing to immerse themselves in what is hopefully a well-constructed story with interesting characters which is the exact same thing they should be doing with professional wrestling. When viewed from this perspective the similarities become quite striking. For example, in both the film and professional wrestling worlds, the script is key. What the characters are doing and why they are doing it become essential to moving the plot forward which is essential to keeping the audience engaged. The actors must then competently and if you are lucky, with charisma, deliver that script. The greater the charisma and the greater the talent, the bigger the superstar. The flip side of course also holds true - if the actor is not able to deliver their lines competently the audience will react negatively towards them. If the story is bland or predictable this will also cause the audience to lose interest. To further the analogy, you can think of the moves and holds in wrestling as the special effects of movies. If the special effects in a movie are bad or cheap or the moves in professional wrestling do not look like they connect or are effective this destroys the willing suspension of disbelief and pulls the audience out of the illusion. Same rules, different medium.

People still go to professional wrestling shows wanting to be entertained and they do that by engaging in willing suspension of disbelief which I hold is essentially kayfabe and they do it for the stories and the characters and the way it makes them feel. By this definition, kayfabe is not in fact dead however it is - by watching modern professional wrestling - ignored. This is the danger of thinking that kayfabe is dead. You see it from backyard wrestlers to Indy wrestling to network wrestling and even in the WWE they have all decided kayfabe is dead and instead of focusing on the stories and the characters, which people will choose to believe in, they seem solely interested in moves, holds, counter moves and counter holds which, as we've already established, is merely a device to communicate psychology and cannot stand alone as entertainment. Continuing our analogy, I've oftentimes heard people say about the movie that it wasn't very good but the special effects were amazing. What they are saying of course is that they didn't particularly enjoy the experience on multiple levels they were merely impressed by the technical accomplishment of the special effects. A quick follow-up question regarding if they would see the movie again or recommend it to a friend reveals a vast majority of them saying "no". Flip the script and how many times have you seen people super excited about a film with great stories, great characters, and little or no special effects raving about it and telling all their friends to check it out? Apply this to wrestling you quickly see that a match with amazing moves but no story and bland wrestlers is absolutely nothing compared to a match that has a great story, great characters a little more than punching, kicking, and a handful of big moves.

A prime example of this failure to understand the concept of willing suspension of disbelief is the world championship belt. It doesn't matter if it is a singles belt or tag team belt the fact remains that modern writers have decided that since people know the winner is predetermined that chasing and/or obtaining the belt is meaningless. They incorrectly believe that since people know that the winner is going to be picked based on some other arbitrary factors that whoever wins the belt did not "earn" it. This reveals a staggering lack of creativity and insight on the part of the writers. When kayfabe was in full effect the championship belt holders were based on who had the most talent, the most charisma, or ideally – both, with the goal of attracting the largest crowds when they performed. While this concept may be difficult to translate to modern audiences, and since the older audiences were not aware of these conditions, it may seem difficult but all is not lost as there are certainly other things that can be done. An additional behind-the-scenes fact of the world title holder was that they made more money than most other wrestlers on the card. This would be a fairly easy concept to sell to a modern audience by leaning just a little bit into their willing suspension of disbelief. Thinking about it for five minutes without fully exploring all the implications, here is a simple idea around the concept of title-holders making more money. You basically establish that the title belt comes with it an additional annual salary of $1 million. It is still not in dispute that the holder of the belt has been predetermined but if you stick to the additional money willing suspension of disbelief allows for many varied and different storylines and motivations that can all be centered around the quest for those additional funds every year. It is no longer the prestige of being the belt holder since everyone knows that is predetermined but it is now the additional monetary compensation. What modern writers fail to understand is this adds some real stakes and drama to the matches regardless of whether predetermined or not since within an engaging story and characters the willing suspension of disbelief is strengthened. It is still a question of whether the good guy will win or the bad guy will win and importantly what the fallout will be from either one of those two winning the match.

Another important psychological fact to know is that people project themselves into the entertainment to vicariously have an experience represented in or by that entertainment. Imagine the myriad of possibilities of programming a wrestling angle where a "Joe average" type works his way up the card and eventually gets a shot at the world title. This hero's journey is at the heart of all great storytelling and, as long as there is sufficient struggle along the way plus personal charisma with the individual, this wrestler will get the average fan very invested in their journey. Culminating in their ultimate victory and winning the title belt they now have "succeeded ". This gets the audience emotionally involved beyond the moves, holds, counter moves and counter holds of professional wrestling that seem solely to be on display in today's environment. It doesn't matter what your role is in professional wrestling you owe it to yourself to familiarize yourself with Joseph Campbell's idea of the hero's journey. It will be covered in detail later but here is a chance for you to get a head start.

A quick note before we dive any further into this. You will see a lot of references to the idea that the goal is to generate interest in the audience so that they pay for a ticket to see the next show. A lot of people will immediately dismiss this saying it is a relic of the house show past whereby wrestlers made the bulk of their money at house shows and that these days, at least at the top, wrestlers have guaranteed pay contracts so they don't need to worry about such things. This could not be further from the truth and is a gross misunderstanding of what the bulk of this book is about. Whether it is to show up next month at a house show or tune in next week for a TV show or pony up money for a pay-per-view or streaming service everything that happens in the ring should be geared toward engaging the audience and manipulating their emotions to get them emotionally invested in the product. Even though some of the things in this book say "in order to get them to pay for a ticket to the next show" I guarantee you that the actions that generate that result will generate the same result for all the other outcomes listed above from getting them to watch the next TV show to getting the pay-per-view ticket to purchasing a streaming service. Don't get hung up on the "old school" situation, focus on the philosophy, the concept, and the actions.

THREE RULES INSIDE THE RING

(and there are only three)

7

Especially if you are a professional wrestler but even if you are a manager or referee or promoter the foundation of professional wrestling can be summarized and understood if you know the only three things that a wrestler should be doing in the ring. To understand how misunderstood this is, and if you want to have a lot of fun, do what I've been doing for many years. Walk into any locker room in any professional wrestling organization regardless of what "level" they are at (sadly you'll get the same result in a WWE locker room) and ask the workers there what are the three rules every wrestler must follow in the ring and inform them that their only three. First, I can tell you that I have never received a correct answer. Second, the answers that I do receive tend to fall into similar categories. There are the answers that they think I want to hear such as "put on a good show" or "work the crowd". There are also "smart" answers such as "follow the booking exactly as it has been presented" or "further the storyline". Sadly I also get a lot of really stupid answers such as "have a good time" or "get my shit in". That last answer is a particularly vexing one as it displays an insane amount of ignorance and disrespect and is sadly something I hear far, far too often. So, what are the only three things you need to do in the ring you ask? Here they are in order of importance:

1. **Protect yourself**

    Don't stop reading just because you didn't like what number one was. Most people I've spoken to expect this to be some grand revelation or extremely detailed secret. Instead, it is the number one rule that, sadly, has been ignored. I don't need to tell anyone reading this that professional wrestling is very dangerous. What I may need to tell people however is that not only are you putting your well-being in the hands of whoever you're in the ring with but odds are, that person has not been trained the proper way. Since there is no way of you knowing this or not what you must do first and foremost and at all times is protect yourself. To give you a real-life example, I regularly trained to be a professional wrestler for an entire year before I ever stepped into a ring in front of a crowd. The first three months of that training were just bumping. I got to a point where I could jokingly bump in my sleep however, I can confirm - and it was recorded - that I did a correct bump falling to the ground after being knocked unconscious. The entire story around the event will help to illustrate not only my point but to give people an idea of how things can go in the world of professional wrestling. The incident took place at the Insane Clown Posse's wrestling show in Detroit, Stranglemania. Things started off wrong when it was revealed that the clowns had placed a gymnastics match on top of the plywood in the ring and then the canvas on top of that. We only found out about this after the first match when the wrestlers came back absolutely livid as such a setup prohibited quite a few things and was quite hazardous as walking or running on such a squishy surface was difficult at best. Regardless, I came out with my tag team in an exploding barbed wire death match. Details of the match are unimportant but what is important is after the match was over I was in the ring when one of the face wrestlers, who previously injured his ankle on that gymnastics mat, in a fit of rage about the injury whipped me off the ropes informing me of a chair shot on my return from the ropes which he delivered with such force that I was instantly knocked unconscious upon contact. Reviewing the video, you can see me still fall correctly, tucking my chin in what is done to prevent you from hitting the back of your head and being knocked unconscious - while I am unconscious. I can say with 100% certainty that it is only because of that training that I am able to write this book here and now. I have seen numerous wrestling schools that spend a couple of weeks on training new recruits to bump and they are doing a disservice to that individual. Tucking the chin and distributing the impact needs to be something that is trained so much and so often that it basically becomes instinct - not even a conscious thought and this needs to be trained prior to ever stepping in the ring in front of a crowd. I so firmly believe in this that I've even floated the idea that bumping should be taught to young children at public schools as invaluable in their life since at some point they will find themselves falling backward or forwards and having the knowledge or more importantly the instinct to land properly will result in not only countless fewer injuries but possibly even save quite a few lives. Nearly every injury and every severe injury save one that I have seen inside a professional wrestling ring was the result of the wrestler not protecting themselves.

There are two components to protecting yourself. The first component is training. Not only must you train to bump properly but you also have to train to take moves, holds, counter moves and counter holds properly. It may sound silly but I have seen someone get injured due to their ignorance on how to take a body slam. A basic and simple move that combines another element of the three things that you must do in the ring however for our purposes in this section, you must learn and understand your part in that move not as someone executing it but as someone it is being executed on. These things can only be learned through repetition and learning them in front of a live crowd should not be an option. We need to kill the idea of working matches in front of a live crowd as "practice". Even though this seems like common sense I have not seen this approach in any professional wrestling school. The reason being is simple, the schools are there to make money not train people to be a professional wrestler. You might think that sounds contradictory but hear me out. Bumping and learning to protect yourself when taking moves is not exciting. It is not "sexy" or "fun". It is called the basics for a reason and schools realize that many students are there solely to do high spots. Those are exciting. Those are "sexy". Those are "fun". The problem is of course that high spots are, by their very definition, dangerous and cannot constitute an entire match - even though I have seen countless wrestlers try countless times to make them an entire match. If you are going to be successful in this business you must be able to instinctively bump, have a vast knowledge of how to take every single move, and have the mindset that at all times you must protect yourself because, sadly, the other person probably will not.

The second component is, for lack of a better term, using common sense. Often times matches will require something more than simply locking up in the ring and executing moves and counter moves. Anytime any element is introduced to a match you must thoroughly analyze it for potential dangers. Arguably the worst injury I have ever seen in wrestling was the result of what is generally considered a routine occurrence - fighting outside the ring. I was managing at the time and the two wrestlers in the match took to the outside and began brawling ending with a body slam near one of the corner posts by the face on the heel that I was managing. Being close and observing the action I noticed that the heel was not moving properly and not selling properly either so I instructed the face to jump in the ring and play to the crowd while I figured out what was going on. I asked the heel if they were okay and they said no they were bleeding in the back of their head and felt "odd". I ran my hand around the side of the skull to the back and to my horror felt my finger go into their skull. A quick examination revealed the following -

for those of you unaware some wrestling rings have screws that stick out of the bottom of the four support posts. A seasoned construction crew will always have these screws facing into the center of the ring. This crew had an oversight that night and the screw was facing outward. The body slam resulted in the heel's head smashing into that screw at such an angle that it broke right through the skull creating a hole. Casting blame at this point is useless since, in all honesty, any one of the three of us involved in the match or a ring crew chief (if one exists) should have done a quick check around the ring to make sure nothing would have been an issue or impeded our ability to fight outside the ring. Granted, we may have missed the screw, but common sense and due diligence dictate that we should have at least made the effort. The more extreme the wrestling match, the more important this becomes. I will contrast two experiences to show you exactly what I'm talking about. As I previously mentioned, I found myself managing a tag team in an exploding barbed wire death match for the Insane Clown Posse. We examined the method that was being used to create the explosion and realize sparks would be flying off as part of the effect. As such seconds before going out for our match we all completely doused ourselves from head to toe in water. It was enough to wet all of our hair and clothes but not so much to where we would be weighted down or dripping all over the ring. This was done to mitigate the risk of our hair or clothes catching on fire from one of the sparks regardless of how remote of a chance there was of that. This was good common sense. Contrast that to a show that I did for Indiana University at a frat house pledge party. We were hired to put on a wrestling show in the backyard of this frat house during pledge week in order for them to stand head and shoulders above all the other frat houses. They wanted it extreme so we were going to deliver. One of the spots planned for one of the matches I was involved in as a manager was for my heel wrestler to be beating up the face pretty good and call for me to set up a table. I was then going to balance a table between the ring and the guardrails, use lighter fluid, and set the table on fire which the heel would then have the face positioned in such a fashion that he would be outside the ropes in front of the suspended table on fire then drop kicked and bump backward into the flaming table. On my side, there were some precautions taken. The table legs were locked in place and not extended so that when the wrestler went through the middle of the table the legs would fall to the side with the break instead of possibly wedging against the side and creating an even split in the table. The lighter fluid puddle that I created to set on fire was nothing more than one narrow stream down the middle of the table. Lighter fluid tends to spread so if using it in a match, less is always better than more. Finally, as I would be the one setting the lighter fluid aflame, I made sure to douse my clothes with water. Everything went according to plan except of course for the fact that the face took no precautions whatsoever despite my instructions. His clothes were dry as a bone and as he hit the table at a bad angle his clothes caught fire. I am not sure what they were made of but they went up quickly. It was so bad all pretense and plans were lost as he started running back into the frat house and I chased after him attempting to find something such as a blanket to put him out with. He failed to protect himself and as a result, walked away with first and second-degree burns on his parts of his body. This conveniently brings us to the second thing you must do in the ring:

2. **Protect your opponent**

Again, I suspect many people are not happy with this second rule. To many people, the first and second rules seem to be obvious. From watching professional wrestling at every level, I can sadly report they are not. It might actually be more accurate to say they are not given the focus that they deserve. As I mentioned in the first rule not everyone is taught to, or has the foresight to, protect themselves - it, therefore, falls to you to protect them. This is accomplished almost solely through training. It is common, but horrifyingly not universal, for trainers to explain to people how when executing a body slam on their opponent they use one of their hands to help tuck the chin of their opponent. How many though will train you how to protect your opponent for every single move you put on them? How many teach you how to land on your opponent while jumping over the top rope to the floor? From my experience the answer is none. A very simple rule to live by is that for every single thing that you plan to do to your opponent you should be aware of something that you need to do to protect them during that move. It is at this point that people start to say "well, that's ridiculous since you can't protect your opponent while you're flying through the air getting ready to land on them". If you've ever watched truly great professional wrestlers who leap off the top rope and come crashing down just fine on their opponent you may notice that they tend to arch their back pulling their arms and legs up to create an almost banana-like position. This is not unintentional. It both looks great to the crowd but also allows them to hit their opponent with the least amount of dangling limbs that could do damage. They can pull them in at the last second to soften the blow and this gives them total control to adjust the limbs depending upon how well the trajectory of the landing is. This is just one of several examples of how with a little bit of thought you can always ensure that you are protecting your opponent.

The word opponent is slightly misleading as it should be protect everyone in the ring. As a manager or referee or timekeeper or announcer, you are not exempt from this rule even if you're not physically involved in the match. A great example of this is from one of my favorite matches of all time that I was involved in. The match took place at a National Guard Armory and if you've never been inside a National Guard Armory they are pretty much the perfect place to run independent wrestling shows as they are large concrete rooms with a high ceiling and they also have amenities such as showers and locker rooms. This Armory had some tall standup lockers that were being replaced so they had set them in the main room. Seeing the potential, I asked and was given permission to use/destroy these lockers. With this permission, we decided the go home for the match was the face jumping off of the top of a locker - which was about 7 feet tall – onto the heel who would be laid out on a table. I was managing the heel so I was close to the action when we reached the time to go home. The face executed an under-hook DDT on the floor which did not look like it was sold properly and then placed the heel on the table and began his ascent to the top of the locker. I was selling an injury but made my way to the table to check in on the heel and confirm that he was ready. I received no response whatsoever. After a second attempt and looking into his eyes I knew immediately that even before the DDT, the heel was unconscious. He was completely unable to protect himself from a 260-pound man flying almost 10 feet up in the air and landing on him as he was laying prone on the top of a folding table. By the time all this registered that 260-pound man was airborne and my only option at that moment, and what I ultimately did, was throw myself on top of the heel and take the brunt of the impact from the face so he landed on me and I was able to protect myself and lessen the blow to the heel under me. After the match and upon further investigation it was determined the heel had been suffering blackouts not only in matches but in his day-to-day activities so this was an issue completely unrelated to the actions in the ring that could have resulted in serious injury as he was completely unable to protect himself or even know what was about to be done to him.

I cannot stress enough how important this concept is as it has been losing favor in more modern times. I have even had some of the more knowledgeable wrestlers claim that this is a relic of a bygone era. The claim is that "back in the day" when the territories system existed wrestlers had the ability to work if not every single night of the year well over 300 times. If they were not working, they were not making money. It was therefore in their best financial interest to remain healthy and injury free. The counter to this is beyond obvious as even though wrestlers are not working anywhere near that amount today that doesn't negate the need to be safe and injury free. Just because you may have a week or two between matches doesn't mean you should spend that time "healing up" but you would be shocked as to how many times I have heard that very claim. Beyond the common sense of staying injury free, there is the match and the story to consider or more accurately there should be. Getting injured at any point of the match affects the ability of that match to tell the story that is intended or to be satisfying to the audience. I lost track of how many matches I've seen where someone clearly got injured 30 seconds into a match or even five minutes into a match and there is clearly much more to be done yet either the match was quickly ended or in severe cases medical attention was provided for no other reason than one or more of the wrestlers involved failed to protect their opponent or failed to protect themselves.

The first two rules basically cover the actions that you and your opponent engage in while in the ring but the third rule has everything to do the philosophy you must have when you step into the ring:

3. Make your opponent look good

This is far and away the rarest thing I have seen in modern professional wrestling. That seems absolutely unreal to me as this is the only thought that you should have every single time you step into that ring. The statement is as powerful in what it says as it is in what it does not say. Nowhere in that statement is the idea that a wrestler should "get over" or "put on a good match" or "draw heat" and especially not the phrase that I hear over and over and over again in locker rooms "get my shit in". Many professional wrestlers do not understand that going into the ring solely focused on making your opponent look good and their opponent also going into the ring solely focus on making you look good means that everyone comes out looking great. I cannot stress this enough as it is honestly an idea and concept that I cannot remember the last time I actually saw it. It is so rare in fact that I had to dedicate an entire section of this book informing you what the roles of the face and heel are and how they act. That chapter will serve to put this idea into greater focus but for right now I need to make everyone understand that this is a mindset that they need to adopt immediately.

Walking into a ring with the sole idea you are going to make your opponent look good and the full understanding they are going to walk into the ring with the sole idea to make you look good is the only way to truly guarantee a great professional wrestling match. There is no room for selfishness in the ring and yet, it is almost all I see these days. Sadly, it occurs to me that I need to define what making someone look good is. You make someone look good by executing on what story is attempting to be told during the match. I saw a recent match that could be used to illustrate in a multilayered way how to not achieve this goal and then

I will give you the breakdown of how it could have been done properly. There was a tag team match and the faces were defined as people who came out and slapped the wrists of the fans around the ring while the heels were defined by coming out and ignoring the crowd and providing terrible insults such as "you suck" with little else. The match was absolutely horrible as it consisted of little more than the faces continually getting one up on the heels after a very brief beat down with no cheating by the heels whatsoever and little selling on the part of the faces to illustrate the heels as any kind of real threat. In the end, the faces easily won and the crowd gave a mild reaction as they had not been sufficiently drawn into the match and there was never really any doubt as to the outcome. There was a short amount of time with the faces celebrating in the ring and the heels giving a silly complaint to the referee when music hit and out walked a tag team from one of the nationally syndicated professional wrestling shows currently airing. These two came to the ring clearly with greater confidence and swagger as they had reached a national level and even did a brief tease as to if they were there to side with the heels against the faces or do something else. It didn't take long for them to show their hand as they quickly dispatched with the heels while the faces stood there and just watched. This new tag team then made a single acknowledgment to the face team and proceeded to take the microphone where they provided one-time lip service to the promotion - not to the face team in the ring - and proceeded to plug their own merchandise which they were selling on a table in the corner. They then left the ring to go sit and sell merchandise. Within 30 seconds or so the face team left the ring to go behind the curtain and everything was over. The entire match and post-match content accomplished absolutely nothing except getting a few T-shirt sales for the nationally known tag team.

It is not difficult to guess what the promoter thought was going to happen in this match. Clearly, he thought that paying money to bring in a national tag team they would work to get over the promotion's existing top tag team as legitimate contenders on a national stage as well as the promotion itself by indicating something to the effect that they were there for the high level of competition provided by the promotion, etc. To accomplish this would be the simplest thing in the world. After a hard-fought match where the faces barely won over the treachery (read: cheating) of the heels, the heels would engage in some post-match beat down relentlessly doing damage to the face team until such time as the music hit and the national tag team came out. Noticing the numbers game had changed the heels would not engage this new team but instead roll to the outside of the ring gloating over the beat down they had just provided. The national tag team would quickly see to the health and well-being of the recently beat down face team then take the microphone and acknowledge the great work of the face team, the dastardly deeds of the heels, and how they had come to the promotion not only seeking the highest level of competition but to right, the wrongs that they saw in the locker room and just could not contain themselves any longer. With proper booking and advanced knowledge of the arrival date, this would have been easily the 4th or 5th beat down by the heels on the faces to really drive home the fact that the heels always cheated to get the upper hand and rarely faced any consequences for doing so. This setup does not provide a direct feud between the national tag team and the heels nor does it eliminate the possibility that they may have to face the face team later in a very uncomfortable situation as booking the national team regularly may not be in the budget for the promotion. The connecting thread in all of this is that all parties involved will be making an effort to make their opponent look good. Since everyone is trying to make everyone else look good everyone is ultimately elevated. In the scenario I provided the face team looks good, the heel team looks good, the national tag team looks good and the promotion looks good. Contrast that with the reality of what happened where the only entity that looks good is the national tag team and it is clearly done by their design with little regard for the promotion or the wrestlers in that promotion.

Arguably the greatest professional wrestler ever - Ric Flair - is the very definition of making your opponent look. Spending most of his career as the world heavyweight champion Ric Flair immediately had credibility as the best of the best. He would use this to his full advantage by going into different territories and entering every match with the idea that he would start out strong but eventually be overwhelmed by the superior technique and/or toughness of his opponent. He would then cheat to win the match or bailout of the match all together. Continuing the concept of making your opponent look good even when not in the ring Ric would then provide an interview where he was absolutely shocked and livid over the fact of him being challenged and/or made to look bad by what he originally considered an inferior opponent and now accepted an equal and possibly superior opponent thus elevating that opponent to a whole new level. He would almost always additionally include that he was shocked that the promotion itself had such high-quality wrestlers thus elevating the promotion. He has been accused of just doing the same thing over and over again in his matches and yet there is a very good reason he did this - it works. Period. The psychology on every level is sound and is the heart of what professional wrestling is all about.

There are no other rules.

Having presented these ideas to various wrestlers, promoters, fans, etc. over the years I've often had them interject and say "well, yeah maybe there are those three but there is also this rule..." 95% of the time this additional rule is self-centered. The most common one is "make myself look good". I accept it takes a certain amount of ego to be a professional wrestler. To be a great professional wrestler, however, requires an equal amount of humility and intelligence. You have to understand that what goes on in that ring requires more than one person. Call it a performance, call it a dance, it doesn't matter but at the end of the day, you're relying on someone else to work with you to achieve a goal. As soon as the focus is placed solely on yourself, achieving that goal becomes that much more difficult or just downright impossible. If you walk into the ring with the goal of making yourself look good and your opponent walks into the ring with the goal of making themselves look good you have a nightmare scenario and sadly, the most common type of match that I see today where two or more wrestlers ignore the crowd, ignore psychology, ignore the story and just focus on trying to do big moves incorrectly thinking that this is what impresses an audience or even worse, solely because they want to impress themselves. It seems ridiculous to have to say that professional wrestling is not a solo sport and yet I see it all the time. The remaining additional rules wrestlers suggest tend to revolve around things that you should already be doing. For example, from time to time I will hear that "work the crowd" is an additional rule. Working the crowd is something you should be doing every match all the time with rare exceptions. An exception example would be if a face and a heel have a nice run where both have been doing their job and the crowd is incredibly emotionally invested then it would make perfect sense in a blowout match for the face to come to the ring hyper-focused on getting his revenge against the heel and ignore the crowd and being "all business" and the heel also being too focused to acknowledge the crowd. You could argue that this in and of itself is still working the crowd but instead, I'll argue it's making your opponent look good. Another counterargument I often hear has nothing to do with an additional rule but the idea that everyone in the ring may not be following these three rules.

What if not everyone follows these rules?

The argument is generally structured along the lines that if everyone is following these rules great but if your opponent doesn't care about making you look good or doesn't protect you then you don't need to follow these rules either and you might look weak if you do. First and foremost, understand that a single match does not make a career. Every wrestler has had a match with an egomaniac where they tried to sell for them and even structure the match with some back and forth but the egomaniac ruined it and just tried to make themselves look good. Outside of making sure you never work with this wrestler again there is little you can do but I have seen some success via education and experience. I've actually sat with two wrestlers going over a match where I was managing the heel and the face said the plan was for him to beat up my guy for about four minutes straight and then pin him. The heel and I were visiting this promotion and clearly got stuck with an egomaniac. I asked if he had seen a match that aired on a national program and he said yes and I pointed out how in that match the face was being beaten up by the heel and when he finally capitalized on a mistake by the heel the crowd went absolutely crazy. I suggested that we try a similar thing here as there was no belt on the line and it was just a standard house show and he would look amazing to the crowd. It took some convincing but eventually, the face relented. We started off the match with the face hot (this was done to appease his ego early on) then a nice crotch shot to the face from me on the outside allowed the heel wrestler to take over. The heel then proceeded to beat on the face regularly including cheating on both our parts and two fake comebacks by the face until finally as a set up to the go home we did the big face come back. It was structured perfectly and the crowd quickly became invested so the reaction to the comeback was exactly as designed and as I told the face it would be. In the locker room post-match, the face enthusiastically declared that he had never received such a reaction from the crowd. A small victory indeed and I didn't work for that promotion or with that wrestler again but I sincerely hope he took to heart the ideas presented and that he started to follow the three rules.

Not everyone is open to new education and new experiences so, regrettably, if you find yourself in the ring with a wrestler or wrestlers who do not follow the three rules first and foremost fall back hard on rule number one. Countless are the times that I've seen wrestlers injure another wrestler while trying to impress themselves. These wrestlers are poorly trained and poorly educated and are a danger to everyone who steps in the ring with them. To my horror, they also represent a very large percentage of wrestlers that I run into. As self-promoting as it seems, I would also suggest recommending this book to them. It may not however be for the reason you think. In my experience the ego of these bad wrestlers prevents them from accepting advice from other wrestlers as they see themselves better than anyone else so short of someone from a national stage informing them, they will not take anyone's advice. Therefore, getting advice and understanding from an impartial book may in fact be the best way to at the very least start the process of them understanding what it really takes to be a great professional wrestler.

8

KNOW YOUR ROLE

(we're all in this together)

9

Everyone inside the ring, and even outside the ring, has a role to play in crafting a great professional wrestling experience for the crowd. Just to be clear, I will not be getting into the minutia of roles such as cameraman, sound technician, timekeeper, etc., etc. Instead, I'll be focusing on the primary roles involved in putting on a great match - wrestlers, referees, managers/valet, and announcers. A great match can happen without all of these components operating at their peak level but each part not working well with the others diminishes the chance of a great match and reduces the overall quality of the match as a whole.

FACE WRESTLERS

The general thought amongst most wrestlers is that the face wrestler is the "good guy" (or girl of course). They think the face is the hero of the story for the fans that they are generally athletic with a smile on their face and pep in their step. What the face really is, is an archetype that fans imprint on during their willing suspension of disbelief. The face is what the audience members generally revere and strive to be - the idealized version of themselves (strong, confident, a "winner"). When the face wins, the audience wins. When the face struggles the audience struggles. This has incorrectly caused many wrestlers to think that being the face entails nothing more than slapping the wrists of fans as they come to ringside and then soaking up the cheers when they win. In reality, the psychology is much, much deeper and specifics are covered in the next chapter.

The face is also considered by many people in the audience as a "friend" or someone they would like to be friends with as they are idealized. One of the most powerful ways to draw in an audience is by engaging them beyond random hand slapping. I have two examples to illustrate this point. On a national stage, and for those that are not familiar, there was a wrestler named Ricky Morton who was part of a tag team that also was somewhat small for a professional wrestler at the time. The formula for his matches that work absolutely perfectly was for the heel team to spend most of the match beating up Ricky as bad as they can with him generally making a hot tag at or near the end of the match to his partner. Ricky was a very good wrestler so he would sell the beating expertly. He did however have one particular move that illustrates reaching out to the audience in a unique and powerful way. Despite needing to project an air of strength and power Ricky simply lacked the size to do this. Exploiting this fact, especially during big blow-out matches, Ricky would have the heel team beat him to such a degree that it looked like he was sure to lose and then put him a hold where, to the audience, it looked like he was being stretched painfully but of course was actually a rest hold. Ricky would make sure that the heel positioned the move such that Ricky would be facing either the audience or a camera and would extend his arm as if he was reaching out to them and mouth the words "help me" and you would instantly see the faces in the crowd drop and on occasion have tears well up in their eyes as they were pulled into that moment and wanted nothing more than to jump into the ring and help their hero poor Ricky Morton. A second example from my own career is watching the crowd file in backstage on a monitor I noticed we had a repeat customer which was a young man in a wheelchair. This was clearly not due to an injury but a lifelong affliction. I got the heel and the face together and told him my plan and so in the middle of the match when the heel was up on face outside the ring I went over and grabbed this kid in his wheelchair and wheeled him into position. The heel then took over and with a running start ran the kid in his wheelchair into the face's side. It was of course done in a manner that looks painful but would not send the kid flying out of his wheelchair or damage the face's ribs. We got backstage after the match and several wrestlers attempted to admonish me for doing that with the kid in the wheelchair. They would say stupid things like "you could've injured him" or if they thought they were smart "he likes the face so he must feel terrible that he would be used as a weapon against the face" and of course the idiotic "I can't believe you did that without asking his permission first". The reality is very simple. When I went over to grab him and wheeled him into position, he could have locked the wheelchair at any point if he wasn't comfortable or "didn't want to hurt the face" and I had a contingency plan for that however he did not lock the chair. Once he was in position, I took a look at his face and the smile told me everything I needed to know. The heel was of such a skill level that I knew he wasn't going to push the wheelchair fast enough to throw its occupant or to do any real damage to the face. What these naysayers did not understand is that by singling out that individual and getting him involved in the match I was fulfilling an audience member's dream. It was not perhaps in the way he thought - whereby he had an opportunity to help the face - but for a brief moment he was part of the show. I also instructed the heel and we made sure that we left the kid in the wheelchair next to the face after being rammed into him so that the face could brace himself on the wheelchair thus making the kid in the wheelchair feel like he did in fact help. Above and beyond all that this kid has a story that he is going to tell every single person who will listen the next day at school/work/home, etc. and possibly for years to come.

As the face represents the audience 99% of the time they should not cheat. Notice I left 1% open and most of the bad wrestlers use this as an opening to be able to cheat whenever they want. The sad fact is almost the only the time a face wrestler should cheat is when doing so in the exact same manner that the heel had done to them on numerous occasions in the past and that will allow the face to win a big match. That's it, otherwise, there should be no cheating by the face. Starting in the 90s, and slightly prevalent today, many bad wrestlers will tell me that they are not a face or heel they are a "tweener". The implication or definition that they use is a wrestler between a face and a heel sometimes cheats for advantage or to win. This of course doesn't exist. Now when presented with that fact they instantly say "you're wrong, Stone Cold Steve Austin was a tweener". It is at that point that I must point out Steve Austin was 100% a face. Why was he 100% face? Because of all that I just outlined. The only time he ever cheated was to throw back in the face of the heel what had been done to him. Sadly, it is at this point some wrestlers will try and point out that Steve Austin punched people close-fisted and that was cheating. Technically they are correct but the closed fist rules is not enforced (there would probably not be professional wrestling if they did) so it really is a moot point. The important takeaway is that there is no "tweener".

HEEL WRESTLERS

Simply put, the heel is the bad guy but more accurately put, the heel moves the story along. We have to start with the basics again as these topics are not generally covered in any kind of wrestling school. The heel is not just someone who comes out and insults the fans, wrestles a back-and-forth match, and then leaves lobbing a few more insults at the crowd as they do so.

A side note on insults must be presented here. Any insult involving a swear word such as "fuck you" or "you're a bunch of assholes" is not only weak and sad but completely ineffective. These types of insults are heard on a daily basis often times in a mocking manner and hold no weight or currency in a match. The other insult I will hear about 200 times at a professional wrestling show from the heels is the phrase "you suck". Again, pathetic. Insulting the crowd is generally done in two different fashions. The most common one heels should rely on is audience-wide insults. Even though it is been done by many, the classic insult of saying "I'm going to introduce something new to this audience it's called soap" works absolutely perfectly as it insults everyone in the crowd regardless of their personal hygiene. It also works from the standpoint that it insults an audience member's friend sitting next to them, family members, etc. Individual insults can also work but it takes some intelligence and quick thinking. If the heel for example is walking to the ring and one fan is particularly engaging then there is an opportunity for the heel to further the dislike by delivering a well-thought-out insult to that individual. The odds are the heel's never seen this person before and doesn't know anything about them so it can be seen as quite difficult. The rule of thumb is to find some physical attribute that you're able to hone in on as not only is the person being insulted aware of the physical issue but the people in the crowd, to varying degrees, will be able to see that imperfection as well. One of the most common issues these days is weight however simply saying "your fat" is not going to cut it as any kind of decent insult. On the flip side, very obvious and demeaning insults also fall flat. Saying something as stupid as "you're going to die alone and fat because no one likes you" will also generate little to no reaction in a crowd or individual. It may sound silly but a line such as "get tubby here a hot dog before he passes out from starvation" works on multiple levels. Identifying the individual as "tubby" reduces them to a description not an individual. Implying that this person needs food all the time because they're always hungry and therefore overweight is all said with just a few words and carries far more power not only on the individual but on the crowd as a whole. A third type of insult is possible if you have some parameters in place you are ready for. I call this "fishing" as you are trying to find one person in the audience to insult and at the same time say something that would insult or offend everyone. A perfect example of this is the insult idea that I had for over a year before the opportunity arose to use it. It may seem odd but the trigger for this particular insult was a baby crying and I went dozens of matches without hearing that sound until finally one day I did. Thankfully it was in the middle of one of my monologues as a manager and while I had no idea the specific location of the crying baby I had a general idea of the area it come from. I immediately said, "stop, stop, stop hold on a second" and made my way toward the side of the ring where I had heard that crying baby. I pointed my hand in the general direction of that crowd and said "I hear a baby crying and I'm telling that mother right now to shut that kid up or I will come up there and shove it back where it came from." Now that insult works on many levels. First and foremost, it is vile without being vulgar or graphic. To clarify - what I state I am going to do is graphic but it is not graphically explained. I have not used a swear word at all. I have keyed into a core ideal for most people, the protection of their offspring, as well as the protection of themselves as what I suggested would harm both to themselves and to the baby. I've also insulted their baby by admonishing it for crying (a natural occurrence). In addition to all that everyone in the crowd immediately leaps to the defense of this poor woman who was insulted and attacked for doing nothing more than having a child which is what most human beings do anyway. Quick note to those of you who have never been involved in a wrestling match inside the ring - if the crowd is large enough you can't make out any individuals whatsoever. This is the case here so I had no ability to ascertain the individual reaction but the "boos" and insults from the crowd let me know that it had hit home. I later found out from security that the actual woman involved handed the kid to her husband and started to make her way down the steps to attack me until security stopped her. That is real heat and that is invaluable.

Getting back to the real function of the heel, which is moving the story forward, the obvious question is how do they do that? The first thing you have to understand is that most people are passive in their life. They are much more likely to allow things to happen to them as opposed to make things happen for them. This is neither good nor bad but something that keys in to how a heel acts. Simply put, a heel does act. That is to say, the heel is the person who engages in some act or activity in order to move the story along. If two wrestlers who had never met have a match and after losing the heel viciously attacks the face to start their feud then the heel acted and created the impetus for a story between the wrestlers to begin. Faces are almost always reactionaries.

Much like the people in the audience they will react to the situations presented in their lives. The "everyman" face is just trying to work hard, live their life decently, and hopefully get ahead by doing so. They live primarily through the clichés of keeping your head down and not rocking the boat. The heel on the other hand is a shit disturber, has no respect for anyone or anything but themselves, and is always causing problems. Using the very basic structure of the storyline feud previously mentioned you'll see that it is the heel that moves the story along in every case. The heel starts the feud by cheating and dishonorably attacking an opponent after a match has ended thus creating the motivation for the interaction between the two parties. As the feud progresses it is the heel for example that costs the face a victory in an unrelated match or leaves the in the middle of a match between them thus depriving the face of their victory and pretty much any and all other slights and offenses that add a sense of revenge that the face, and therefore by extension the audience, will ultimately achieve. The face doesn't run around interacting with and instigating things with the heel since even though that is something that audience members would like to be able to do in real life, they don't, and having the face do it might provide a small sense of satisfaction but it does nothing more than diminish a large amount of satisfaction at the end of the feud. It is the sole responsibility of the heel to be constantly provoking the face which is effectively moving the storyline along. As with all things the rule is not 100%. Once the face has been sufficiently motivated by consistent disappointment and failure, they may be prompted to instigate their own act or action that this should be limited to one or possibly two times over the course of a feud and there should be significant time between such interaction and the final blow out in order to restore the cathartic enjoyment of victory in the final match.

It is also a general rule that the heel is the one to call the moves, holds, counter moves and counter holds in the match. For the most part, the face should be concerned and focus on selling the beating and engaging the crowd. When done properly this allows the heel to judge the crowd response. I say when done properly because again I rarely see heels acting the proper way in the match. Certainly not after every move, but certainly after a big move or after cutting off the face the heel should always, and I mean always, interact with the crowd and at the same time determine how over the aforementioned action got. The result from the crowd then determines how things progress from there. This is obviously called reading the crowd and is almost a dead art from everything I've seen and yet it is one of the single most important skills that any wrestler should strive to learn and perfect. To illustrate this, I was managing the heel in a promotion with a regular show in a small town where we main evented every single show for about six months (the heel/face feud we were in was ok, but we made sure no one was going to follow our match entertainment wise). The match styles were hard-core and we made a point to be as creative and different each and every time. We came to the ring one night and for some strange reason were met with a chorus of cheers and applause. It wasn't just some isolated pocket of idiot smart marks, it was a majority of the crowd. We upped the insults without much luck and even started the match with plenty of cheating and behind-the-ref-double teaming that did not sway the audience. I told my guy to execute a big move on the face and let them know to sell it for a couple of minutes so we could try something different. I grabbed the microphone off the announcer's table and stood outside the ring ropes on the ring and taunted the crowd that they like us, they like what we did, etc. which was met with some unwanted cheers. I then informed the crowd that we were not there to amuse them and we had other means and tactics to achieve our goals so I told my heel wrestler to execute plan 174 (obviously a made-up number) but before he did so to come over so I could give a little secret and when he did, I informed him that until the finish he should wrestle "boring" with lots of basics and rest holds and regular bailouts to the outside of the ring. As soon as the hard-core and creative wrestling stopped and the boring wrestling stepped in, the anger and the booing from the audience quickly followed. It is that sort of the read of the crowd that the heel should regularly be doing while beating the crap out of the face. Every so often you will find yourself faced with a crowd that for whatever reason is just off that night and you need to be able to adjust midmatch to match the vibe of the audience to get them engaged and send them home happy or better yet send them home dying to buy a ticket to come see you again because they're so pissed off at what happened.

MANAGERS/VALETS

I put these two together in order to point out the fact that they are quite different and yet most people will lump them in together. In today's modern wrestling roles can often times blend together but when done properly there should be a very clear distinction.

Traditionally the valet has been female and very attractive. This is done by design as the role was one of not only eye candy but also a source of distraction. Furthermore, the valet is generally received by the audience as a "weaker" individual. It doesn't matter what modern sensibilities or political correctness is currently ascribed to these ideas the fact remains that if those core concepts are maintained you could have a very effective valet. For the sake of simplicity, I'm going to utilize the male/female dynamic here. Recall much of the appeal of professional wrestling for the audience is projection. With that in mind, the moment a wrestler walks out of the locker room with a valet psychology kicks in. If the wrestler is a face then the audience members projecting on to them feel happy about being with such an attractive woman while on the flipside with the heel, the audience is jealous and further dislikes the heel from being able to get a girl that they can't. The condition on this of course is that the girl with the heel must not be a heel. Remember the audience is supposed to dislike the heel - if the heel is doing their job correctly - so the goal here is for the audience to like the valet in order for that dynamic to exist with one exception. The distraction factor is very powerful and can be used in a variety of situations. The heel can menace or threaten violence against the face's valet thus causing the face to be distracted from the goal of winning the match in order to defend the valet. Either the face or heel wrestler can become romantically enamored of the female valet, etc., etc. Remember that exception I mentioned before? You can have a heel valet for no other reason than for the face to become romantically enamored with her and eventually turn her into a "good" girl. This is of course done by nothing more than having her not cheat but it does provide ample storytelling opportunities. The valet appearing to be "weaker" also helps with the distraction. It is one thing to split the attention of the wrestlers but it is quite another when you have the classic "damsel in distress". The reason that archetype works is that every man wants to be the hero to someone and as they are projecting on the face when the face swoops in and saves the defenseless valet from the evil heel you have a simple but effective and proven to be an impactful storyline for the audience. The last condition for the valet is that they never get involved unless there is absolutely no danger for them whatsoever. A very simple and basic example of this is a story whereby the heel has been quite lecherous and inappropriate but never successful with the female valet and then in a match, the heel is beaten up to the point where they can't defend themselves so the face holds legs open and the female valet gets to kick the heel in the crotch. Simple but effective and not something that should be dismissed just because "it's been done before". Always keep in mind everything has been done before, it is merely how well you present it and what subtle changes you make along the journey.

    A manager is something quite different than a valet though clearly sharing some of the same aspects. They can be used as a distraction and they should definitely be perceived to be "weaker" - a wrestler and their manager should not look like a tag team. That is about as far as the similarities go however since managers not only can but should, get physically involved in the matches. There is a cliché that there's no such thing as a face manager and I would have to agree with it. The moment a manager becomes involved in a match in the audience's mind it effectively becomes a 2-on-1 situation which is not fair and not fair is the purview of the heel. It doesn't matter if there's cheating or even if it's justified, as soon as a manager gets involved the equation changes. A great rule of thumb to further explain the differences between the two roles is the valet should always be a face and a manager should always be a heel. Having the ability to physically interact also opens up a myriad of storyline possibilities. Heel managers can cost the face the match, accidentally cost their wrestler a match, cheat to turn the tide of the match, or provide comic relief such as in the scenario where they are forced to step into a tag match when one of their guys is missing and of course is a great temporary satisfaction for the crowd when the manager gets beat up and since it wasn't the wrestler being pinned, you still have that for the crowd to look forward to. A great example of the last two situations I can relate from personal experience. I was managing a tag team for some time but for one of the shows only one of the guys didn't show up. Their car had broken down on the way to the show so technically it wasn't their fault that they were not able to be there for the show. I came out for the match with my one wrestler and explained to the crowd that the other wrestler had their car breakdown and would not be there tonight so there would be no match. Any excuse that I gave would not be believed by the crowd as I was the heel manager with the heel team so why not simply tell the truth? As I began to walk back towards the locker room the promotion Commissioner grabbed the mic and told me if I didn't come back that my team would forfeit and lose the match. This wasn't a title match or anything important so I told him fine no big deal no real loss for us. The commissioner said I signed a contract and it was all about giving the people what they wanted so since I didn't care about my team losing the match if I didn't come back then I would be banned from ringside in the main event title match at the end of the night. Absolutely livid I went back to the ring and started to scream at him that it wasn't our fault, what exactly did he want me to do about it as I was only managing the tag team and the heel was going to be in the main event so I didn't have anyone to substitute and I wasn't going to have that heel wrestler wrestle twice on the same card when they needed to be fresh and at a hundred percent for the title match, etc., etc. The Commissioner said I had to come up with a substitute and if it wasn't going to be a wrestler then it was going to be me which of course the crowd loved since they were sensing, or more accurately hoping, that this would be their chance to see me get beat up. We did a little back-and-forth false teasing but of course, in the end, I relented and became a reluctant partner in a tag team match. Earlier in the night backstage, we laid out the match in broad terms such that the heel wrestler on my team would beat up one of the face wrestlers really well then tag in me whereby I would come in and either kick them on the ground or drop an elbow and immediately tag back out. A quick side note here to display the psychology at work. That exact scenario just mentioned establishes that I, as the manager, am basically a coward since I don't stay in the ring past one move, I am not a wrestler or even really knowledgeable fighting as all I do is kick or drop an elbow - which is the most basic of moves - and that my heel wrestler is not given adequate time to catch his breath which will come into play later in the match. My heel wrestler was instructed to start selling exhaustion after a couple of exchanges in order to set up the scenario whereby I'm tagged in and I go to drop an elbow but the face rolls out of the way. I sell the elbow as on top of everything else I am also wimpy while my heel wrestler is on one knee facing the crowd outside of the ring heaving his chest selling that he has to catch his breath as he has not been given the opportunity to rest during the 1 move time I am in the ring. The face makes the hot tag and I make my way to the corner but my heel wrestler is not able to accept the tag thus allowing the fresh face to cut me off and begin executing moves on me that rather quickly resulting in a pin and victory for the face tag team. If you're wondering why my heel wrestler can't come in for the save remember he was never given an opportunity to rest so he is still selling the exhaustion in the corner.

The manager also can continue to play the role they were originally invented for, the mouthpiece of a wrestler that doesn't have any mic skills. From the dawn of wrestling, you didn't have to be the total package. In fact, it was more common that a wrestler would have a great look or great in-ring abilities but no skills on the microphone as that is an entirely different skill set. A simple fix to that was to pair that wrestler up with a manager that lacks the size and skill to be a wrestler but can work the mic and get across storylines that way. One thing I see today in the wrestling world is a violation of this concept as once again ego rears its ugly head and you will find wrestlers that demand they must also work the mic. The audience then has to ask the question if this wrestler has it all then what do they need a manager for? I've even had wrestlers debate me over the fact that The Four Horsemen, who were all very good on the mic, had a manager in the form of JJ Dillon. The answer is simple, storyline and character. The Four Horsemen were presented as not only the best of the best but the most wealthy and extravagant of wrestlers around. It, therefore, makes sense that they would hire a thinking manager to handle their business affairs and also clarify or reiterate points in the storyline that needed to be made.

One of the strongest abilities of the manager is to act as an outside observer to the match going on in the ring. Any wrestler will tell you when they step into the ring the crowd effectively becomes a blur. Even when pausing to acknowledge the crowd, it is still difficult to make out individuals but more importantly, it is impossible to gauge the reaction of a crowd while executing the match. This is where the manager steps in and I have found myself on more than one occasion informing the wrestlers that, for example, a string of submission moves is not resonating with the crowd or the crowd on this particular side of the ring is particularly hot so the next time you dump out of the ring dump over there for the greatest reaction, etc., etc. I like to think I coined the term the manager as the thermometer. They can gauge how hot or cold the crowd is, the wrestlers are, what they are doing is, and how the match itself is going over. I'll explain a little later the responsibilities of the referee role but their role tends to end once the wrestlers are outside the ring as the referee should be inside the ring counting them out (barring a no-count-out match of course). What I will say is that once the wrestlers are outside the ring the manager will take over some aspects of the referee role.

I made reference to and will mention several times throughout this book, the high value placed on the idea that you can provide temporary satisfaction to the crowd by having them beat up a manager while still maintaining their interest in seeing the heel wrestler be beat up at a later date. If you have quality wrestlers and you have time to build up a storyline, you must be sure to incorporate this at least once if not twice. The flip side of the coin of course is I will often see the manager beat up every single match which is also a bad idea as it removes any impact or interest the crowd may have in seeing the manager be beaten up since it always happens. The example above with me being pinned after being forced to take part in the tag match is absolutely perfect since the crowd is very happy that I got beat up and pinned but still want to see the wrestler-on-wrestler match with, as they always hope, the faces going over again but this time against the "real" opponents. This touches on a topic of some debate amongst promoters around the country, the idea of always sending the crowd home happy. Primarily on an indie level, the idea is that you're only doing a show once a month in a particular location so in order to keep the interest of the crowd the last match of the night needs to "send them home happy". Most promoters simply think that this means having the face win which is of course the wrong way to think of things as the story must always come first. The manager provides a nice workaround to this. In the simplest of scenarios, the heel wins the match by cheating, and after a short amount of time of the heels gloating the face gets up and attacks the heel usually with a weapon of some kind to put the heel out of commission temporarily and then through a set of circumstances the face finds themselves in the ring with the heel manager where they then beat up the heel manager thus sending the crowd home happy. As I said this is a point of debate and some promoters are more than willing to end the note on the heel victory so philosophical argument or not this is yet another way to utilize a manager.

Speaking of utilizing a manager, the sad reality is that many wrestlers simply won't. Bad wrestlers, which make up over 90% of the wrestlers, have their egos threatened by a manager and will therefore not include them in the planning of the match or merely offer them a one-time interaction thinking that will appease them. Such wrestlers are weak and insecure. I just pointed out numerous ways that managers can be utilized and to ignore that is foolish. To illustrate how a great wrestler handles a manager I was working a sold show at a county fair with Doink the Clown (Matt Osborne) as the headline attraction. I was managing the heel for that match so backstage we set up a spot where Matt would be positioned over the bottom rope, arms spread out and I would come by and pull on his head thus choking him while the referee was distracted by my wrestler. Nothing really much else was planned. The spot came rather quickly so I ran over cupped my hands and gave just enough pull-down to make it look good and allowed Matt to do the selling of the move which he of course did and stopped immediately after I broke the hand cup. I paused for about a second then gave him a pulled slap that did not make the crowd happy nor did the gloating that I did afterward. It wasn't too long after that that I noticed Matt arranged himself to be in that prone position a second time. I walked over and got close enough to hear him say "again" to which we then went through the sequence a second time. The match continued and then I saw Matt arrange himself in that position the third time. At this point, nothing had to be said so I walked over and did the choke and fully expected to happen exactly what happened which was him blocking my slap and hauling off and punching me with his other hand which I sold like crazy. The point of all this of course is to illustrate that a wrestler of Matt's level understood the value of the manager and utilized it to the fullest to create a far better match for the audience by utilizing a simple, but effective sequence.

Another thing a manager may be used for but is extremely rare must be properly set up and used with caution is the idea of a manager as a weapon. The manager must obviously be trained as a professional wrestler and trained well. When utilized properly however it can really add an extra layer to a match. I'll give you a couple of examples I was personally involved in to give you an idea. The first was a scaffold match that I was involved in whereby at the finish a table had been set up just in front of the scaffold (which I should mention was a good 20+ feet off the ground) and the face had beat up my heel wrestler to the point where they were laid out prone on the table. The face then quickly ascended the scaffold since there's nothing stupider than slowly climbing a scaffold or ladder thus giving your opponent plenty of time to recover but they don't because you have a spot set up. But I digress. Seeing what was about to happen to my wrestler I ascended the scaffold on the opposite end at the same time and pace. Reaching the top at the same time, I begged and pleaded with the face to not jump off the scaffold and land on my wrestler to which they "replied" by kicking me in the gut and then throwing me off the top of the scaffold so that I would come crashing down on my wrestler in the ring on the table. A great bit of insult to injury for the crowd to eat up which of course they did. The face triumphantly played to the crowd. While he was doing that, I rolled around selling the pain but in reality, turning myself over so that my back was on the chest of my heel wrestler so that shortly after the face pointed down to us and got the acceptance from the crowd they could jump and came splashing down. The second example is a move that we actually did in a few different places but it requires a wrestler with very good positioning. The basic setup is that the heel wrestler I was managing beat up the face to the point where they were laying on the mat about halfway between the rope and the middle of the ring. My heel wrestler would position themselves at the midpoint of the ring facing away from the face behind them. I would then enter the ring, run to the ropes in front of my heel wrestler and when I got towards them, they would position me for a powerbomb but instead continue the momentum all the way over their head such that I would come crashing down chest to chest on the face behind the heel wrestler. A very good heel wrestler would even spin and come crashing down on the mat with me for further impact. Obviously, the possibilities are limitless if you have a heel manager that is also trained as a wrestler but keep in mind that the moves should not be considered super big since a heel manager is perceived as smaller and weaker by the audience. In the scaffold example, the heel wrestler was not pinned by me landing on him but by the face landing on both of us. In the powerbomb example, it was not the pinfall setup move it was merely just one of many moves executed against the face prior to the set-up of a big move or the pinfall itself. I would also limit such moves to one per match and infrequently amongst repeating crowds. Rarely do crowds see managers used in such a fashion so to maintain a high level of impact they should be used sparingly. I'll give you one more example of me being utilized as a weapon. I was managing a heel wrestler who was completely jacked. He was in insanely great shape and strong as an ox so this move was actually possible. He was battling outside the ring with a face, and executed an underhook DDT that temporarily knocked the face out. He then returned to the ring whereby I entered it and we both goaded the referee to count the face out for our victory. The face was coming to and made their way almost to the guardrail so, as was planned in advance, the heel wrestler stepped outside the ropes still on the ring in the corner and taunted the face to stay down. The face was now up about to step over the guardrail when I climbed to the top turnbuckle from inside the ring, my heel wrestler then pressed me over his head throwing me into the face technically still in the crowd. This of course broke the 10 count but was effective since it looked like the face was going to make it back to the ring in time but more importantly, was a devasting move.

REFEREES

Without question, the referee is the most overlooked and underrated asset in that ring. Most wrestlers and promoters I meet think the referees are there for nothing more than to count the pinfall or sloppily take the bump when they're supposed to. The reality that should exist, but I admit does not, is that the referee should be revered inside that ring as long as they themselves understand their value and utilize it. Referees should be the eyes, the ears, the communication medium, and the arbitrator of the mechanics of the match for the wrestlers. For example, in a properly structured wrestling match after a big move is executed the wrestler executing the move should then acknowledge the crowd. The referee should check on the wrestler selling the severity of the move. Most referees will check on the physical condition of the wrestler asking if they were hurt but great referees will also occasionally check the stamina and ask for any instructions to convey. The logical step as far as the audience is concerned after a big move is executed and the wrestler has been checked on then the referee would go to admonish the other wrestler for doing the move or for ignoring the match (depending upon heel/face structure). This is where messages can be conveyed much better than when locking up or when whipping into the ropes as those are times when communication from a ref would seem strange to the audience thus breaking the willing suspension of disbelief. In addition, as you'll see later, referees should be in the corners for most of the match, not in the middle of the ring where wrestlers are whipping each other off the ropes. In the absence of a manager, the referee can also gauge the reactions of the crowd though this does take away from their observation of the wrestlers. I've even seen the referee be used as a conduit for providing and then hiding a blade. Bottom line is that great wrestlers take full advantage of having a 3rd party in the ring that is not directly engaged with them thus allowing them to solely focus on what they have to do. At the same time, the referee should not be afraid to tell a wrestler when it is time to pick it up or if a certain move or style is not working. They can tell them which side of the ring is hot or where some idiot smart marks are in the crowd to avoid, etc., etc. The list of ways the referee can be utilized goes on and on and yet is consistently overlooked by wrestlers, promoters, and even the referees themselves.

ANNOUNCERS

To be clear I am not referring to a ring announcer who says the height and weight and names of the opponents but instead to someone who announces over the matches in either a play-by-play or a color commentary capacity. Announcers either in front of a live audience or especially when announcing prerecorded footage have a unique power that cannot be overlooked. Quite simply put they have the power to make a bad match or move look good, a good match or move look great and a great match or move look epic. Since I have no idea what year someone will be reading this book, I implore you to seek out and find matches where the announcer is a gentleman by the name of Jim Ross. He is without question or argument the single greatest play-by-play announcer of all time. As soon as you have done that seek out matches where there was an announce team that consisted of Gorilla Monsoon and Bobby "The Brain" Heenan. Bobby Heenan is without question or argument the single greatest color commentator of all time. You would think logically combining Jim Ross with Bobby Heenan would result in the greatest announce team ever but Bobby had better chemistry with Gorilla. Either way, watching any of those matches you will quickly understand just how powerful the announcing can be. The psychology is heavy at work here since the announcer in a way becomes the conduit through which the audience experiences the match. Yes, they are physically there watching it on some media so they are able to form their own thoughts and opinions, and views yet having an announce team allows them to vicariously experience it in another way. When the announcer is excited, they are excited. When the announcer is surprised, they are surprised. That alone is a great power but it is not solely what an announcer can do.

There is a cliché about soap operas that is generally considered to be true and that is that you can start watching a soap opera at any point in time and within a week or so be fully up to speed on everything that's going on in every one of the characters' lives. As wrestling is the male soap opera this should hold true for wrestling as well. The announcer is what makes this possible. They have a lot of filler during the match so the excellent announcers will take the opportunity to recap some events that have brought us to this point in the storyline or remind the audience about a previous slight or injury that may be directly impacted by what is going on currently in the ring. Announcers are the ones that fill the gap and are able to do the exposition the wrestlers are not.

One of the best things that you get with great announcers is the ability to flesh out or expand upon the current storyline. With first-hand knowledge of everything going on in the promotion, the announcers will be able to recap, emphasize, remind or instruct the audience on the various twists and turns of the current storyline unfolding in the ring. Remember the example I gave earlier where I was forced to be in the tag match where we made sure that I was only in from one move after each tag out? If you watch that match after our amazing announcer got done with it, he made sure to point out first that it seemed like my wrestler wasn't getting much of a break. Then he commented on how it didn't seem like my heel wrestler was getting a chance to 100% recover after the tag. He then followed it up by asking the question how is the heel wrestler continuing without that much rest then commented on how the heel wrestler was slowing down finally speculating that if this continues the heel wrestler will not be able to tag back in at some point. If those thoughts and ideas were not going through the mind of the audience while watching the match they were once those statements were made. The color commentary portion of the team can also help out with this greatly. They are generally a heel as that affords them the greatest opportunities to flesh out characters and storylines by how they describe the wrestlers and the action. Defending the cheating of the heel and downplaying the talent of the face is not only the standard operating procedure but has been proven to be very effective. The audience automatically distrusts the heel and psychologically assigns the opposite of whatever they say to the individuals they say it about. If the face executed a perfect dropkick and the heel color commentary says it looked like it was weak the audience will feel it is much stronger than it possibly was. Color commentators are also great at providing some comic relief. Remember the audience is there to have fun and laughing is fun. Once again, I direct your attention to Bobby "The Brain" Heenan as he was the undisputed master of this. He knew when to insult the face and exonerate the heel and was also infinitely skilled at dropping humorous lines including self-deprecating ones that made him look bad as he was a heel manager. I am not sure it will resonate without the visual but we had a tremendous color commentator and part-time heel manager who was doing the commentary on a match that had in the match a different heel manager. This heel manager was an overweight individual that was known to talk for far too long and far too much. The color commentary, as soon as this heel manager was on screen simply said "oh look, it is the round mound of sound". Perhaps you had to be there but the entire crew working on that recording fell out laughing like you would not believe.

Another incredibly useful ability that great announcers have is to hide things. Even at the highest levels, the best professional wrestlers in the world run the risk of missing a spot. The law of averages alone suggests that this will happen to everyone at some point. The clever announcer can cover up a blown spot quickly with a simple phrase such as "oh, a glancing blow" or "looks like he misjudged his positioning ". The audience knows the mistake was made but if they have a quick little something to fill that gap willing suspension of disbelief returns.

10

PSYCHOLOGY IN WRESTLING

(the male soap opera)

11

The best way to endear an audience to a character is to utilize the hero's journey made famous by Joseph Campbell. In its most basic form, there are 3 steps. A fully realized arc will contain 12 steps. This is important to note especially in professional wrestling as it provides multiple storyline possibilities which are important since unlike a book or film there is not one hero's journey the face must go through but a non-stop series of hero journeys. This also provides a great instructional blueprint since someone fresh out of wrestling school or with a minimal amount of time in the industry who finally lands at a promotion where they will be performing for a long period of time or even indefinitely can start the simplest hero's journey and then build from there. An essential point of the hero's journey is that not only must it be utilized in storytelling but it must also be utilized while crafting a match which is covered later in this book. For now, let's look at the two different levels of the hero's journey and how they relate to a face wrestler.

3 Steps –

1. Departure
2. Initiation
3. Return

In film, television, and books the departure stage is generally defined by the hero leaving familiar surroundings. It is generally a homestead as the hero is generally young and just starting out their life but the familiar could also be a long-time career, a family, a location, or any other established norm for the character. The departure stage represents the beginning of growth and change. This isn't translatable per se to professional wrestling unless this is the first time an audience is meeting a wrestler then their "journey" has already begun. If the wrestler is already established with this audience due to repeated exposure a change in character or a new feud with the heel can also represent this departure. The important thing to translate to the audience is that something is about to change in the face's life.

The initiation stage is by far the most important and the easiest to translate into the wrestling ring while at the same time being the stage that is most often overlooked or incomplete. The initiation stage is where the hero struggles, repeatedly fails, and ultimately triumphs. What I see most often is a heel will attack a face - ideally after a match - provide a small beat down of which the face ultimately recovers a little bit to run off the heel and this is supposed to pass as the initiation (or at the very least the beginning of it). It happens this way since, once again, neither the face nor the heel really understands that they are supposed to be working a crowd and telling the story but instead are only concerned with how they look. If you're going to follow the scenario properly, a great way to do it is as follows:

The heel and the face have a match that is structured properly (see the section of this book on how to do that) with the face just barely manages to get a win with a superior technical move. After a brief moment of celebration where it would be believable that the heel has time to recover from their injuries and the face has had time to acknowledge the crowd the heel would attack the face from behind - it is extremely important to be from behind since heels must cheat - and then proceed to beat the holy hell out of the facr. This would be a long beat down with the heel making sure to let the crowd know exactly what they were doing. The face would not get any comeback whatsoever, no one from the back would come out to save them and the referee would be the first person to be ejected from the ring by the heel. After a thorough beating, the heel will smugly acknowledge their superiority, and walk to the back and thus the initiation stage has begun. The next part of a properly structured journey would be repeat matches between the face and the heel whereby the heel always wins by cheating or loses in a way that does not settle the issue between the two such as a heel accepting a count-out loss in order to avoid the superior skills of the face.

The return stage for professional wrestling is more symbolic than literal. The end of this journey is represented by the face's ultimate triumph over the heel in some large and well-built-up match. They return not to their original place of origin but they return to a point where they will have to start the journey all over again with a different opponent in order for the crowd to be continually engaged.

12 Steps –

1. Ordinary World
2. Call to adventure
3. Refusal of the call
4. Meeting a mentor
5. Crossing the threshold
6. Test-allies-enemies
7. Approached the inmost cave
8. Ordeal
9. Reward
10. The road back
11. Resurrection
12. Return with the elixir

Though this may seem daunting, any clever promoter with talented wrestlers and a consistent show with a repeat audience can attempt to tackle the full hero's journey. There are of course an infinite number of stories and options for each 12 of the steps so I will use one of the most famous and perfect uses of these steps in the story of Magnum T.A.

and Mr. Wrestling 2 crafted by one of the greatest bookers of all time - Bill Watts in Midsouth wrestling. To set the stage at the time of this Magnum TA was very green and had a good look but not a lot of skill. Mr. Wrestling 2 was a respected seasoned veteran nearing the end of his career but still a viable worker in the ring.

Step 1 - ordinary world. This is generally where the hero starts and it establishes them in their everyday normal life and where the audience gets to know about them. As previously stated, this may or may not be possible depending upon the exposure of the wrestler. In this scenario, Magnum was a new wrestler to the area and he was presented as the All-American clean-cut good guy with good wrestling skills but honestly not a lot of character.

Step 2 - call to adventure. In professional wrestling, there is by nature of the sport always a call to adventure. Generally, it is either the next match or, prior to the late 20th century, the quest to achieve a title belt. In Magnum's case, especially as he was just starting out, it was merely the next match and establishing himself in the promotion.

Step 3 - refusal of the call. In this specific case, there really was no refusal to call. For context, a great use of this would be a situation where a heel viciously attacks a face that used to be his friend and the face refuses to fight back. The call to action would be to defend oneself but the memory of the friendship caused the face to refuse that call.

Step 4 - meeting a mentor. After seeing the efforts of Magnum T.A. in an interview Mr. Wrestling 2 pointed out that Magnum had the skills but lacked a certain something that would take him to the next level and offered to mentor him and guide him on his journey.

Step 5 - crossing the threshold. Magnum accepting the offer of Mr. Wrestling 2 is his switch from his ordinary path to the new one which will take him to greater heights.

Step 6 - test-allies-enemies. The promotion did a brilliant job of not only showing Magnum getting better in the ring but also included videos of actual training with Mr. Wrestling 2 which is in effect testing him and along the way, they discover who some of their allies and enemies are. Most importantly it is during this stage that the seeds are planted for the ultimate betrayal by Mr. Wrestling 2 as not only does Magnum progress quickly but even becomes good at Mr. Wrestling 2's signature move – the knee lift.

Step 7 - approach the inmost cave. After improving and winning and losing matches it is becoming apparent that Mr. Wrestling 2 is the real challenge that Magnum must overcome. This is incredibly difficult as Mr. Wrestling 2 is his mentor and a great friend but Mr. Wrestling 2's jealousy and ego continue to be a source of brewing conflict.

Step 8 – ordeal. The final inner crisis that Magnum faces is the inevitable battle between him and Mr. Wrestling 2. There is always a death associated with this stage and in this case, is the death of his friendship and the father image that Mr. Wrestling 2 represents.

Step 9 – reward. Even though the North American Heavyweight Title was on the line the reward that Magnum received was also him maturing into a better wrestler, getting revenge against the misdeeds of Mr. Wrestling 2.

Step 10 – 12. As stated by the very nature of professional wrestling the show must go on. A wrestler does not have the luxury of enduring the road home, overcoming the final metaphorical battle, and finally settling down back into ordinary life but changed and is better than when they left. Magnum was changed and better than when he left but the next journey either already begun as there were multiple storylines going on same time based on the matches he had during this journey – as there should be.

Utilizing this system with either the 3 steps or even variations of the 12 is a tremendous foundation to begin to understand the psychology of what's going on in the ring. Another concept of almost equal importance was mentioned before and that is the willing suspension of disbelief. The willing suspension of disbelief is granted by an audience member to the performance upon consumption of the product - in this case, the performance in the ring and/or the stories being told. The "world" in which a story takes place can be considered its "canon". This basically creates the parameters for what will and will not be accepted by the audience. For example, if a movie takes place in 500 BC and people are seen using cell phones the canon is broken and the audience is immediately taken out of their willing suspension of disbelief. While that is a very obvious break there are more subtle ones that most often occur in characters or in the basic understanding of how the world works. To understand how breaking the rules of how the world works if a movie that doesn't contain any superheroes or special abilities but has somebody fall off a 10-story building, stand up, and walk away, no one in the audience is going to believe that because they understand in that world, a.k.a. the "real" world, that person would be if not dead suffering from quite a few broken bones that would make them unable to walk. As for character rule breaking if you establish a character as being extremely intelligent and resourceful but then show them as being stupid and them struggling with a basic problem that the audience can solve that character loses all credibility.

This shouldn't have to be said but professional wrestling takes place in the real world. Don't stop reading! Yes, everyone knows that, and yet almost every match that I have seen in the last 20 years has absolutely ignored this rule. So how are wrestlers ignoring this rule? Simple, they refuse to acknowledge and accept that people get hurt when they get hit. For the most part, watching wrestling these days is watching a wrestler badly sell being attacked while you can see in their eyes and actions they are just waiting until it is their "turn" to do the attacking since they foolishly think this is what makes them look good. Someone who is being attacked especially for a prolonged period of time is not going to instantly have any pain and be able to fight back. It does not make sense to the audience as they know that in "real life" when someone is hurt it takes a while to recover. This concept can be stretched certainly. There is really nothing better than a heel beating down a face for 4-5 minutes straight only to have the face counter with some big move that results in both of them requiring some time to recover. It doesn't technically make sense that the heel needs the same amount of time to recover from one move that the face needs from a four-minute beat down but the audience is willing to accept this in anticipation of the excitement of the face getting their revenge on the heel. Simply exchanging short periods of executing moves on your opponent until it is their "turn" is the absolute worst way to conduct yourself. That being said, it is not simply enough for a heel to beat up a face for the majority of the match. As far as the audience is concerned it is not the "how" of the beat down but the "why". What moves the heel executes or how bad the beating is pale in comparison to the hate and disdain that must be displayed by the actions of the heel. Furthermore, the story should provide some motivation as to why the beatdown is occurring. The face could hold a title belt, the opponents could be former friends, there could be a love interest triangle involved, or any other infinite variety of reasons for one person to go against another. The one "reason" that is not acceptable however is that they are fighting because one is bad and one is good with no other "reason" whatsoever. Even if two wrestlers have never wrestled before and it is the beginning of a feud that has no external reasons whatsoever by the end of that match the heel should have cheated and stolen the match from the face to a degree that at a bare minimum the face desires justice for being denied the victory. That would explain part of why they are fighting but there needs to be more subtle actions on the part of both to further engage the audience. A great way to engage them is for the heel while beating the face to taunt the audience, berate the face verbally, get in the face of the referee and all around be an uncooperative, rude, and insensitive asshole. The more the audience dislikes the heel the more vested they are in seeing what they hope will ultimately be the victory of the face. On the flip side, the face must make sure that the audience believes the beating is real and that they are in real danger of losing not only the match but their reputation as a skilled and competent fighter. Their job is to sell the beating while at the same time maintaining their honor, not cheat, and after a couple of false starts, relying on their superior skill to if not win the match, then to continue the story. They are not there to come out and to the best of their ability execute moves and holds to display their technical prowess. This actually works against them as the audience does not appreciate a braggart or show-off. Remember the journey above? Combine this with the fact that the face is what the audience is imprinted on and understand that their lives are viewed by themselves as a struggle so overcoming obstacles is much more appealing and engaging than just being the best automatically without any effort.

The actions inside the ring are extremely important and they should always be designed to move forward the story going on outside the ring. By its very nature professional wrestling is not only escapist entertainment but like a soap opera continues on and on without a clear beginning, middle, and end as you would find in a book, or film. There is no easy or simple way to explain or educate someone on how to write good stories for professional wrestling. As a testament to how difficult it is, there are only a handful of individuals that have ever been recognized as truly great bookers – Eddie Graham, Bill Watts, Paul Heyman, Jim Cornette, and Kevin Sullivan are the only names that quickly spring to mind (though there are others). As a side note, you will notice one name that is most definitely not on that list and that would be Vince McMahon. It is arguable as to what Vince McMahon is good at (many would say nothing at all since everything was given to him by his father) but storyline writing or being the booker is not one of them. The only time that the WWE/F ever had great storyline booking was during the attitude era which was done by a committee of bookers including the aforementioned Jim Cornette and I suspect it was almost all him. Others point to Dusty Rhodes or Ole Anderson as great bookers but they were more concerned with booking themselves to look good than booking good storylines. When crafting good stories, you have to take into account two things - the character of the wrestlers involved and the ability of the audience to relate. To make a clear illustration of this let's look at one of the greatest storylines ever which was the Steve Austin and Vince McMahon feud during the height of the attitude era. The core idea of the storyline was the common everyman getting one up on his asshole boss. This idea is insanely relatable to nearly everyone in the crowd as most people do not like their boss and/or think that they know more than their boss or are better than their boss. Giving them the ability to vicariously experience getting one up on their boss by having Steve Austin do it is a stroke of genius. Also, a stroke of genius is having Steve Austin the character do it. The Steve Austin character was the everyman - or more accurately an idealized everyman. He didn't take crap from anyone, stood up for what he thought was right, was a little out of control, drank beer, and had a sort of "I don't care" attitude. Nearly everyone in that audience could relate to that and imprint on him making him the most perfect choice to plug into that storyline. If for example, they had tried to make the snobbish rich educated Hunter Hirst Helmsley the "everyman" who went after Vince McMahon it would have failed miserably as few in the audience would be able to relate. Another great example would be the previously mentioned storyline with Magnum TA and Mr. Wrestling 2. Magnum as the rookie wrestler needing guidance and Mr. Wrestling 2 as the grizzled old veteran immediately fit perfectly into that mentor/student storyline (and just to be clear that storyline was given to us courtesy of Bill Watts). The trick, if there is one, is to key in on thoughts and feelings, and experiences that most people have. The love triangle is a classic in professional wrestling to which many people in the audience can relate. The reason that heels can draw so much heat by beating down faces after cheating is that most people consider themselves honorable at least to a certain degree (aka I wouldn't do that). To give you an idea of how you can exploit this there was a great angle in ECW (courtesy of Paul Heyman) whereby one of the wrestlers named Gary Wolf was in a real-life accident and broke his neck. The angle would have worked whether it was broken in real life or not just for the record. Gary was involved in a feud with a wrestler named Shane Douglas and obviously, the broken neck put the break (so to speak) on their feud. At some point, after recovery, Gary did an interview wearing "the halo" which were steel rods on top of a harness that forced his head to stay in place while the neck heeled. Shane Douglas interrupted this, eventually grabbing Gary by the halo, and threw him to the ground. This is one of the greatest heel moves of all time to such a degree that the fans legitimately rushed the ring. This keys in to most people's desire to not pick on or further injure the already injured. It is considered a weak and cowardly move that most people do not see themselves capable of as only the lowest and most despicable person would even consider such actions. Now of course in real life Gary had been cleared a week prior to removing "the halo" as it was not needed any longer and he just kept it on for this particular angle. A good booker will either ask themselves what they find to be good about themselves or what would be seen as good in others and uses that to craft storylines. Harder than it sounds I'll grant you but as I said before there is no simple plan or outline for writing good professional wrestling storylines. Study psychology, study human behavior, and watch professional wrestling shows that were created by the great bookers listed above. Like a great painter or novelist, you can always learn from the masters.

12

TRAINING MECHANICS

(you're not being taught correctly...or at all)

13

Every Professional wrestling school that I'm aware of is fundamentally set up the same way. They get a new student to cough over some money and then either put them through some cardio and strength exercises that cause many to run away or immediately start to train them how to bump. If they have the strength and cardio first then those who stick around after are moved into the learning how to bump stage. This stage is without question far, far too short for what it should be. As I stated previously, I trained for an entire year before I ever stepped into a ring in front of a crowd and much of that year was bumping. I don't say that everyone else should have a similar timescale out of jealousy or bitterness but because, as I have also previously stated, learning to bump to a point where it almost becomes instinct saved my life on more than one occasion.

Regardless of whether bump training is short or for an appropriate time the schools then will traditionally move on to the basics. This again is an area where far, far too little time is spent. The basics are generally presented as the easiest way to start a match - the lockup, the go behind, the reversal, etc. what I have never seen utilized properly is the fact that these moves set the table for what will be a contest of skill. If the audience sees two wrestlers engaging in "the basics" they will understand that this is the foundation for what would then be a match. On the flip side what I usually see is the bell ringing and the two wrestlers doing at best a quick lockup then someone throws a punch and the high spots begin. What that sort of sequence does is completely bore the audience. Many wrestlers will argue with that statement saying that the crowd is cheering for the high spots so they must be in to it. They are of course applauding the acrobatic skill of high spots but that does not mean they are not emotionally invested in the outcome of the match which is supposed to be the goal of all wrestlers inside the ring.

After the basics are over (that is operating on the idea that they are taught at all) the training quickly progresses to bigger moves such as body slams, pile drivers, suplexes, and more. If you're lucky you'll be taught how to protect your opponent while exercising these moves but more often than not no such education is provided. What I also see generally taught at this point is nothing more than this is how you throw a body slam. What I do not see is the instructor saying "okay, after the body slam the person being slammed is to sell the impact of the move so the person throwing the body slam can acknowledge the crowd". Instead, these impact moves are generally presented as just something you do as part of all the moves that you do. Again, this is where canon is broken. To the people in the crowd, if someone is picked up flipped head over feet, and slammed hard onto the mat they should be injured or have the breath knocked out of them or whatever. The point is they would need some time to recover from such a move. Instead, what I almost always see is immediately they are grabbed by the hair, picked up, and set up for the next big move. Rinse and repeat until such time as it is the other wrestler's "turn".

The express train on training continues and now the trainees come up with some sort of "finisher" or even more complex high spots for trainees to engage in. If it didn't happen before this is generally where the injuries start racking up. The injuries are not necessarily permanent or life-threatening but as trainees continue to try more and more difficult moves the margin for error increases and the deterioration of the body begins. Sadly, I've spoken to several school owners and trainers and they have said this stage is gotten to rather quickly owing to the fact that most students are signing up for this portion of the school. They are not interested in putting in the hard work and learning everything meticulously from scratch, instead, they just want to learn basic bumping and then how to do big high spots. For many students, if they are presented with the idea that they will have to do a lot of work before learning the "fun" stuff, they will just quit thus costing the school money. It is a bit of a Catch-22 as I fully understand the schools need to make money but this is balanced against the fact that poorly trained and quite frankly dangerous individuals are being turned out of these schools which is not good for anyone.

For most schools I am familiar with this represents the bulk of the training. You will get some help in laying out a match with the skills they taught you and if the school is affiliated with a promotion, you may even get some preliminary matches. In fact, students are almost always guaranteed the matches since what I have heard far, far too often from the schools is that they "felt obligated" to put trainees in a match since the trainees had paid them so much money. Again, absolutely no regard for the safety of the wrestlers or concern for the enjoyment level of the crowd paying money. There used to be a great place for well-trained wrestlers to start to get some exposure and that was in the form of "dark" matches. They were called dark matches since they took place at the beginning of shows before the cameras were rolling. This was of course with the national promotions. What was also understood by the crowd, and made clear from the beginning, was that these were in fact young up-and-coming wrestlers thus lowering the expectations of the crowd and making them understand that there are not going to be story-lines created that they would have to follow. I did it in my promotion and I fail to understand why other promotions don't simply announce 10 minutes before the show is scheduled to start announce that there is going to be a dark match of recent trainees. This is not something that happened every show but if I had some green wrestlers that needed to get some experience in front of a crowd without messing up the main show this was an effective method.

The following is a list of things that every wrestling school should be teaching. I emphasize the word "should" as I've never seen a school teaching all of these things and the schools that have taught some of them rarely do it properly. You will notice that it appears I am repeating myself from some of the information contained in the "know your role" section. I do so on purpose but I also expand upon the ideas here so understand this is by design and intended to be emphasized to get a point across.

1. **Character Development**

    I've devoted an entire section of this book to character development so that should give you an idea of how important it is. Nonetheless, rarely, if ever, have I seen schools that will spend a considerable amount of time on this or to be honest - anytime at all. They generally ask the student what their character is and let them roll with that without truly analyzing if that is the best character and they certainly don't teach the how or why of character traits. If you haven't already please make sure you review the section of this book on character development is that goes into far greater detail.

2. **Selling**

    For reasons I completely fail to understand nearly every wrestling school that I am familiar with operates on the idea that everyone knows how to sell when they walk in the door and therefore, they don't have to be trained on it. They seem to just say to themselves "well, everyone's been injured in real life so just act like you're injured". Selling is more than just grabbing the part of your body that was supposed to be hurt and grimacing your face. Again, I turned to Ric Flair as the poster child for how to do things right. Time and time again after a face executed a high-impact move - something as simple as a body slam – he would not only grab his back and grimace his face in pain but also arch his back severely and then spin around, get on his knees and beg the face to not hit him again. This was not only selling the move but also selling the superior skill and power of the face. An example of selling wrong is something I see often in a match where a wrestler is working a single body part in order to set up something at the end of the match. Even though it makes sense that as you are continuing to damage a body part it should hurt more and more, I almost always see the same selling technique on the first damage to the body part as on the 20th damage to the body part. I've only seen it done a handful of times but one of the greatest selling techniques that puts over not only the injury but involves both parties selling well is as follows: it starts when, for example, a heel works an arm on the face. The face has a handful of false comebacks whereby they attempt to use the arm possibly to throw a punch or move and fail. The reversal is not due to the heel cheating in this instance but in the face selling that the heel has done so much damage to the arm that it is, in effect, useless. Taking it a step further the face has an opportunity really connect with the crowd if they use the opposite arm for offense during a successful reversal as this displays their determination, creativity, and willingness to do whatever it takes to succeed which are traits the audience likes to think they themselves possess. There also is little to no training on overselling, underselling, and no selling. If the match is just started and you get hit sending you flying out of the ring and you cut yourself to start bleeding you have done a disgusting amount of overselling and the crowd is not going to believe it thus breaking the willing suspension of disbelief. Now I accept that is an exaggeration but it illustrates the point that the selling should be commensurate with what the audience perceives would be the amount of damage from a move or series of moves. Overselling is actually rare but I do see it from time to time as there is no real training to prevent it. Underselling on the other hand is rampant. After every single move, there should be some time provided to sell that move. I don't know how many times I have seen someone get body slammed, then picked up and suplexed, then picked up and thrown off the ropes kicked in the gut then power bombed only to a dragged to the corner and get smashed by the other wrestler jumping off the top rope and then getting a two count on an attempted pin. Absolutely no one in the audience believes any of that past the first body slam did any damage whatsoever as it was never illustrated that the first move did some kind of damage much less the second, the third, the fourth, etc. No selling is something that is also rarely if ever used properly. Most of the time that I've seen it these days is the result of ego and not because it serves a purpose in the match. If two wrestlers are of equal size and one decides to no-sell the moves of the other without any real reason then it is just ego and sadly I have seen this on more occasions than I can count. There are times when no selling amongst equally sized components is appropriate. Jerry "the King" Lawler and Hulk Hogan are two wrestlers that, after being beat up (for short time in Hulk's case) would feign an adrenaline rush and no sell a few punches from the heel before executing their big finishing move. This made sense to the crowd since it represented the idea that the face had finally reached a breaking point after being "abused" for so long and they were not going to "take it" any longer - which are ideas that they would like to aspire to in their own life. The other place where no selling can be perfectly utilized is when there is a disparity in size between the wrestlers. Incorrect or not the perception from the crowd is that the bigger you are the tougher and more powerful you are. There is absolutely nothing worse than watching a 6' 8", 325-pound wrestler sell for a 5' 9", 180-pound wrestler. I don't care how skillful or popular the smaller wrestler is there would have to be an extraordinary reason that they would ever be able to do any damage or gain a win over the significantly larger opponent. It doesn't even have to be height or weight either. When I was training to be a professional wrestler my training partner was an individual named Jeremy. Jeremy was tailor-made to be a great professional wrestler. While not over 6 feet tall he was almost

6 feet thick (joking of course but you get the idea), absolutely oozed charisma, picked up on the physicality of wrestling quickly but also had the mind to really make him a great wrestler. At the time I could not be a more polar opposite. I was 5' 9", weighed 140 pounds, and the only charisma I seem to ooze was negative however I was able to handle the physicality and most certainly the mindset. Midway through the training I pulled Jeremy aside and said: "let's be honest no matter what move I execute on you or how hard it looks like I'm hitting you no one in the crowd is going to believe that I could ever realistically do any damage to you". I then decided from that moment on my training would be protecting myself and taking bumps while helping Jeremy learn and perfect moves, holds, counter moves and counter holds. The point is that the ability to inflict harm on your opponent needs to be within the realm of the possible to the average individual in the audience. They don't know the nuance of professional boxing training or mixed martial arts or the physiology of the human body they simply size up (pun intended) the wrestlers in the ring and determine if one could pose a credible threat to the other and for a larger person to ignore that and start selling for a smaller person breaks the willing suspension of disbelief.

3. **Interviewing / Mic Work**

    Interviewing and mic work are so key to moving forward the storyline that I'm appalled by the lack of training given to this key area. Mic work can come in a variety of forms depending upon the level of promotion you're working at. You may be limited to a microphone in the ring but if you're lucky you may be able to have a recorded interview or possibly even be involved in skits. No matter what options are available you have to have good mic skills to truly succeed (or be paired up with a great manager but that's covered in a different section).

THE LOST ART AND SCIENCE OF PROFESSIONAL WRESTLING

I. In-Ring Mic Work

When cutting a promo inside the ring there are a few things to consider. First, the audio is probably not going to be very good due to most likely poor acoustics in the building. As such, it is best to use simpler words spoken clearly and at a slow to standard pace. Multi-syllabic words tend to get lost and speaking quickly causes words to run together. Make sure to project your voice and not yell into the mic. This is so important on every type of mic work and yet what I mostly see (or more accurately hear) on the wrestling scene is yelling. Screaming into a microphone does nothing more than distorting your voice. Projecting is the way you raise the volume. If the match and interview are being recorded be sure to be aware of where the camera is at all times. After saying that I need to point out a problem that I frequently see. There is of course an audience in the building and yet many times wrestlers will stare at the camera while they're cutting their promo inside the ring. This effectively removes the audience from the interview which of course is not the desired result. The best course of action is to acknowledge and involve the crowd throughout the interview with the exception of key elements of your speech. If a challenge is being issued or there is a particularly effective insult or plea of support from the fans this should be directed to the camera to ensure maximum exposure as the people in the audience still get it even though you are not looking at them directly but it directly impacts the people watching it at home as you are directly speaking to them. If you're also just staring at the camera and you are a face, at some point everyone watching in the crowd and at home is going to wonder why the heel doesn't just sneak up behind you and blast you in the back of the head. Feel free to move around that ring and always have something allowing you to see where your opponent is in the ring. You need to be aware of everything going on in the ring as well as the audience in attendance and the crowd watching at home when cutting a promo inside the ring.

II. Backstage Interview

Backstage interviews provide some of the best chances to move a story forward. The obvious advantage is that if you mess it up it can be done again and again since unless you're involved in the WWE as of 2022, I doubt you will be doing live interviews backstage. This is your opportunity to think and plan in advance what you're going to say. I do not recommend writing a script and I'm also keenly aware that at a certain level (the year 2022 WWE at bare minimum) you will be provided a script that is the exact opposite way of how interviews should be done. So, without a script, there should be key ideas or concepts of the storyline you wish to get across. You should have an outline of how you will communicate going from step A to B to C. Outside of that everything should come up spur of the moment and most importantly be directly in line with what your character is all about at their core. Anything that doesn't move the story forward should be eliminated. You must always have in your mind what the audience would respond to. For example, if a face has recently lost a title belt to a heel and is getting a rematch, they could simply cut a backstage interview saying to the heel that they are coming for them and the belt on such and such a day at such and such a time and that they better be ready for the match of their life or something to that effect. It works on a surface level but what would be even better is if the face acknowledged that they were beat on such and such a day and give the heel a little bit of credit for their win (to further establish them as a credible threat), then state that their daddy taught them never to be a quitter and that life is hard and will knock you down but the measure of a man is if they stand back up and so on and that on such and such a date at such and such a time they are going to stand up, not be a quitter and take that belt back. Nearly everyone in the audience has received advice from a parent/parent figure (good or bad it doesn't really matter in this context) and everyone in their life has had setbacks and strived to overcome them. Knowing the face is doing the exact same things that they would do – or want to do as they are imprinting on the face - succeeds in strengthening the bond between the wrestler and the audience and cause the audience members to be more vested emotionally in the outcome of the match. I would be remiss if I did not mention movement. I've seen quite a few interviews where the wrestler/manager was moving all around succeeding in nothing more than having them either move out of frame or denying the viewers a focal point. I got some of the greatest advice on this ever during a limo ride to an airport from the wrestler King Kong Bundy who told me when it comes to moving around in interviews, make sure to stand moderately still (not stiff) and if movement is needed, the camera can do it for you.

III. Skits

Skits are some of the most fun that you can have outside of the ring but only if they're well written. These also require the highest level of acting ability so to be 100% honest they're not for everyone. When considering a wrestler for a skit there needs to be a lot of honest evaluation and the wrestler or the director or the promoter has to have the ability to say the acting level is not good enough and we are not going to do this. Sadly, I have rarely seen that level of honesty and insight. As to the idea that skits must be well written, it would be impossible to give any advice on writing skits as they need to be 100% tailored to the character of the wrestler or the nature of the storyline being told. It is also not within the purview of this book to cover acting skills. What I will say is that, unlike TV and film acting, skits are an occasion where you do want to look straight at the camera. The reason being is the willing suspension of disbelief for professional wrestling does not extend to the idea that there is a magic camera capturing some activity voyeuristically as there is in film and TV - for most films and TV the actors are not supposed to know their part of a production. In wrestling, on the other hand, the audience knows that there is a human with a camera shooting what is going on so to ignore that breaks the willing suspension of disbelief. Looking straight into the camera acknowledges that the camera exists so such an action makes sense. Skits are not designed to be short films but instead a way to present something about the character or the feud that cannot be done in the ring or through an interview. The most classic example would be where a face leaves the building only to be surrounded by fans whereby the face warmly greets them and is signing things when the heel attacks them from behind and beats them up severely. At the end of the beating, the heel should acknowledge the camera insulting the face further and/or the crowd watching. Simple but effective and most importantly moves the storyline along.

4. **Being a referee**

I can safely say never in my travels have I ever experienced a school that trains people on how to be referees correctly or in most cases, at all. From my experience referees will of course be told that they need to know what the finishes are in matches they are involved in but they won't be told what their role is and how they can add to a match on a tremendous level. First and foremost, referees should understand the concept that they are not part of the show. Let me be clear on this as they are part of the wrestling match but they are not part of the entertainment show. When someone wanted to be a referee in my promotion, I would pull them aside and give them some detailed instructions and education on what is expected of them. The first thing I would tell them is that they should primarily find themselves standing or crouching in one of the four corners with their back to the turnbuckle unless there is something going on between the wrestlers that they need close examination on such as a headlock during a rest hold. When a referee is in one of the four corners that is the least amount of obstruction that they will provide to the crowd. As soon as a referee is standing next to a wrestler or walking around close to them, they are blocking the view of a number of individuals in the crowd. This is an example of how they should not be part of the show. Next, I would explain to them that while they are in the corner, they are to be the eyes and ears of the wrestlers in regard to the crowd. When wrestlers are doing their moves and holds and even when they are acknowledging the crowd, they actually don't have the ability to key in to the mood or sentiment of the crowd and have no ability to key into any single member of the crowd. When I was a referee and therefore what I trained referees to do was gauge how well the crowd is reacting to what is going on in the ring. This was not something that had to be communicated constantly but I would frequently in a match see that, for example, a heel would be working a body part and doing it rather cleanly without much communication to the crowd that this was a truly painful experience so I would tell them that working that body part in that style is not getting over. Depending upon the people in the ring I might suggest the heel cheat more, the face to sell better, submission holds are not being understood by the audience or to move on to something different. The referee is the one able to focus on a single aspect of the crowd. Perhaps there is an old lady in the front row who is incredibly into it. Or perhaps there's a group of smart marks in the third row attempting to ruin things for everyone. Communicating such information to the wrestler gives them the option of incorporating things into their match based on the referee's input. An example would be that the face, while currently up on the heel, drags the heel over to the old lady in the front row the referee informed him was super in to the match and invites her to slap the heel in the face. Such things go over insanely well with the crowd and would be missed without the ability of the referee to identify such opportunities. Part of the reason that I was able to do this was the fact that all wrestlers in my locker room are told upfront that the referee is an integral part of the match and that they were to listen to them during the matches. This was done because sadly many wrestlers are either taught or pick up on their own this idea that referees are there to do nothing more than false 3 counts and finally the pinfall. This is sadly an incredible waste of the value that a referee can add to a match. In the absence of a manager, the referee should also be utilized as the determiner of the well-being of the wrestlers in the ring. If the heel throws the face over the top rope to the floor the heel should be gloating to the crowd while the referee goes to check on the condition of the face. Should something be wrong the referee is the one easiest to communicate this to the heel possibly with instructions for an early go home or count out or other alteration to the planned finish. Getting back to how a referee should not be part of the performance, and even though the following concept is broken constantly, I will stand firm that the referee should only be a part of the performance when they are being bumped for a reason. Acceptable examples of this would be the classic bump that occurs when the referee is too close to the action and accidentally gets hit so they are knocked out of action even if only temporarily or the even better example of when a disgruntled heel, after losing a match, punches the referee. What is not acceptable is when a referee either fights back or takes a technical bump from a move. As for fighting back the referee should always be the smallest and weakest person in the ring physically - and as you saw in my previous story regarding training since the referee should not be a credible threat under any circumstances to a wrestler. It doesn't even matter if it is a wrestler in training who has some size and is acting as a referee to pay his dues or filling in for a no-show, etc. It is a mental construct in the audience's eyes that the referee is solely there to do their job and not to fight back. Referees taking any bump outside of being punched or kicked or accidentally hit and falling to the ground completely destroys the willing suspension of disbelief. Canon in professional wrestling implies that these are trained professionals working their craft. The referee is not supposed to be an equally trained professional. Therefore, the referee should not be able to take a perfect bump off of a powerbomb for example. The other reason that they should never do this is that part of the willing suspension of disbelief is that these moves and holds hurt - possibly a lot and in a greater proportion based on disparity of size. Therefore, if executed by a very large individual, the move would effectively break a small referee. Though I have seen it countless times, it is absolutely insulting when a heel gives a choke slam to a referee only to have that referee return two matches later on the card. With my promotion, there was a golden rule that after a ref bump that referee is not seen by the crowd again at the very minimum for the duration of the show and then depending upon the bump in the storyline possibly weeks or months after. It shouldn't have to be said that when a referee is body slammed by the heel in the second match of the night, they should not be out as the referee during the fourth, sixth, or any other match on the same card.

5. **Being a Manager**
Let's be honest everyone wants to be a star wrestler. Getting into this business without a little bit of an ego is a recipe for disaster. Getting into the business with too much of ego is far worse but we won't get into that. Although they have fallen out of favor in recent times, the professional wrestling manager is one of the most essential and dynamic roles in the sport. Traditionally when a professional wrestler did not have mic skills or was playing a character who didn't talk or only spoke a foreign language a manager would be utilized to "speak" for the wrestler. In modern times all wrestlers are expected to be able to do mic work. This of course has robbed the sport of some amazing talents because being a solid wrestler with an incredible amount of charisma and intelligence in the ring doesn't guarantee good mic skills. Even in modern times though, the manager has an amazing amount of utility in the ring. For starters, when there is a manager, they take over the role of wrestler welfare checker from the referee since it makes more sense to the crowd that the manager would be close to the action and involved with the wrestlers. Should something go wrong the manager can communicate directly to the wrestler they are managing and then communicate to the referee who can get the message to the other wrestler. Additionally, while the referee is focused on the crowd the manager has the ability to focus on the wrestlers. Much like a coach in a boxing match, the manager of the heel wrestler for example could determine if they were cheating enough or not and encourage the wrestler to do it more if they're not. A manager trained to take bumps has the ability to fulfill another essential role. When I was a manager, I did the following countless times and it always worked - at the beginning of the show, I would come out with my heel wrestler and insult

the crowd, insult the face, and put over my heel wrestler. I would not be seen again until the final match of the night where I was involved as the manager of the heel. After tons of cheating and interference, the face finally gets me in the ring and executes a move or two on me which would ultimately allow the heel to take advantage from behind and win the match or we would reverse the sequence, and after the heel gets the pinfall the face would get a few shots in on me. This accomplished goal of giving the crowd a "happy" ending that evening since the "dastardly manager" was punished for his vile words while at the same time ensuring that they would come back next month because they still have not seen the face get a definitive win over the heel. Simply presenting a match with the face going over the heel denies that second opportunity of pulling in the crowd. This is utilization of the manager in a very basic and yet effective form. If the manager is very well trained you have an opportunity for a double payoff to the audience. An example of this is as follows: I was involved in a program between my heel wrestler Madman Pondo and face wrestler Ian Rotten. They had a nice series of matches that always involved me interfering either to just cause issues or to even cost Ian the match. It was finally determined that there would be a match where if Pondo won, Ian would leave the promotion and if Ian won, he would get five minutes in the ring alone with me, the manager. This storyline provided equal motivation for both parties to sign on to such a match. Normally in wrestling history anytime a face got five minutes with a manager they might get off a move or two but then the manager's other heels would always come out from the locker room and attack the face mostly owing to the fact that the manager was not trained sufficiently to safely and convincingly bump. As this was not the case with me during this big blowoff match, which drew extremely well, not only did the crowd get the satisfaction of Ian winning over Pondo but we gave them a full five minutes of Ian beating the hell out of me including the announcer doing the "10-second" countdown to the end of the five minutes which we planned and perfectly executed with a shirtless powerbomb onto a 6 foot cactus in the ring. The result was an insane crowd reaction and a red stripe down my back for a few weeks as a reaction to the poison in the cactus needles. A smart booker understands the possibilities that a third individual in, or most cases outside of, the ring brings to the table. Here is yet another example: I booked the following sequence of events as an exercise. The last match of the evening was going to be an over-the-top-rope elimination Battle Royal with the winner to be crowned the new champion for a convoluted set of circumstances booking-wise leading up to this. I was managing the top heel in contention for that belt who was in the match prior to the Battle Royal as well – a "punishment" for previous offenses. During the "before" match I attempted to handcuff the face to one of the ring ropes but they reversed it and ended up handcuffing me to one of the top ring ropes. The match ended with the face going over so the crowd was happy but there remained the issue that I was handcuffed to the top rope since the face had thrown the key into the crowd so I was stuck there. The show must go on and our "commissioner" stated I was now a participant in the Battle Royal so I was "fair game" to be beat on. There were several spots involved where faces could take cheek potshots at me and even a nice comedy spot where I attempted to eliminate myself by dangling by my chained hand from the top rope - my feet remaining an inch above the floor. The end of the match saw me having been beaten up so badly by the faces that I was slumped down in a corner arm raised still handcuffed to the top rope while the remaining two participants in the Battle Royal were my top heel from the "before" match and the top face of the promotion. They battled each other back and forth and finally in a perfectly executed spot eliminated each other. Owing to the fact that I was handcuffed to the ring and could not be eliminated this left me the sole participant, winner of the match, and new champion. There are a few things that can be done after making a manager champion but none of them should be that the manager defends the belt a single time. The audience should know without question that any face in the organization, even a rookie, could beat up that manager therefore there is no question as to the outcome of the match. Yes, you have a bunch of interference and cheating by the heel wrestlers but it accomplishes nothing more than diminishing the value of the belt. After the match was over, the ring crew came down and cut me free from the handcuffs. The face returned backstage in disgust while I grabbed the microphone and instructed my heel to come into the ring. I then arrogantly cut a promo telling my heel and the audience that I was a lot braver and tougher than any of them thought and that I was going to be a fighting champion and the greatest champion in the history of the promotion. I sold it as best I could then went over to the table where the figurehead of the promotion sat, informed him that I was ready to defend my title right then and there and if he would sanction the match I would throw out an open challenge. The crowd of course was extremely excited figuring I was a complete idiot and that the top promotion face that just left would return to enact revenge. The figurehead agreed and I immediately said I'm issuing an open challenge and then my top heel in the ring accepted just as the last word out of my mouth was uttered. This caused some confusion and excitement in the crowd as they thought they might be seeing the heel turn good against me. I then got into the ring and on the mic so that the audience could hear me, I informed my heel that I would lay down for him and he could be champion and defend the belt because I was too pretty to possibly be messed up in a wrestling match by him as he was so vicious and powerful. He immediately accepted so I laid down on the mat and he pinned me 123 then we proceeded to celebrate like we had just won the Super Bowl. The top face eventually came out and ran us off. The roller coaster ride that we provided to the audience was not something that could be replicated with anything but a manager. Let's break down the psychology of everything done here. During the "before" match the audience is upset that I'm constantly interfering. When I'm about to handcuff the face to the rope there is a real concern because if that happens the face will not have the ability to win the match and will basically just be a punching bag. Reversing that scenario accomplishes not only relief in the crowd that the face will be able to continue but the additional joy that I, as the manager, have been effectively removed from the match as I'm handcuffed to the top rope. When the face throws the key into the crowd, he is symbolically giving them power over my freedom which is a tremendous psychological trip to send the crowd even further into joy in not only am I stuck but they symbolically are the ones who control if I ever get set free or not. Once it's decided that the show is going to go on even with me handcuffed to the ropes and a participant in the match, the crowd is once again overjoyed that I'm going to be in the situation where any and all of the faces can take advantage of my predicament. There is of course the comedy spot of me trying to eliminate myself – but being unable to as my feet can't reach the floor - and we make sure that many of the faces did get some cheap shots in. By the time it's only the top heel and top face left in the ring since I've been slumped in the corner for a while now many of the fans forgot I was even there or solely have their focus on wanting the face to win this match and become champion by eliminating the heel then "easily" eliminating me. The double elimination is a disappointment to the crowd as their face did not win however it very quickly dawns on them that I have won and I am the new champion which is absolutely mortifying. This is quickly replaced by the fact that they know I'm a small weakling so even though I'm champion it's only going to last till the first time I get in the ring with any face. Demanding the open challenge from the figurehead makes the audience think that I'm a real idiot and that their face hero is going to accept the challenge and become champion like they wanted to in the first place. My heel quickly accepting creates some mild confusion and hope in the crowd that he might be turning. As for my actions, instead of just laying down and taking the pin it is important that I inform the crowd and my heel wrestler that that is exactly what I'm going to do since then it isn't that wrestling is fixed it's that I'm making a conscious decision to pass the belt to a heel that I manage. This further infuriates the crowd as the heel gets to be champion without actually winning the match to be champion or defeating the face and the face has a rightful claim that the heel is an illegitimate champion. Having the face come out to run us off sends everybody home a little bit happy but mostly wanting to return to see what happens next. All of those ideas and desired emotional responses were considered and planned weeks in advance prior to executing that short angle. Don't think for a minute that this would be considered an anomaly. This amount of thought and preparation should go into every book decision you make and even if you are not the booker, a smart wrestler will always say "what if we did this…"

6. **Being a Valet**
Contrary to some modern schools of thought, a valet is very different than a manager. Generally, the valet is a very attractive female who has no wrestling training whatsoever and oftentimes is the "real life" girlfriend of the wrestler. Sadly, most of the time their entire role consists of walking to the ring with the wrestler then sitting or standing ringside, and walking back to the dressing room with the wrestler afterward. This is a rather huge waste of what can be a valuable asset in the ring. Granted, if the valet is extremely attractive that in and of itself is enough to draw in

a certain segment of people but why not try to draw in more? One of the classic uses of the valet is in a love triangle angle. It is cliche and yet it never fails to deliver when executed properly. It requires time and a well-thought-out resolution but the role can only be filled by the valet. The other great use of a valet is when they do something unexpected or out of the ordinary. We had the prototypical "real life" wife, who walked to the ring and did nothing then leave type valet for one of our wrestlers and after a little over six months of seeing her being bored even backstage, I inquired as to the issue. She rightfully stated that she loved her husband but it was insanely boring just walking down to the ring sitting there and then walking back. She wasn't trained to bump and didn't want to learn and wasn't even sure of what she wanted to do so that she was not "bored" but she was lucky as I had an idea that I knew was sure to get over. The wrestler that she was with was mostly a utility wrestler and not on the top of the card as he wasn't very good but fortunately, a couple of months from when I spoke to her there was an opening match with him and a relatively new heel that I had just started to manage. I moved the match up to just before intermission to test out the idea I had for her. It was basic and just required a small amount of training on her part. I started the match by insulting her character with such gems as "in the locker room we call her the doorknob because every guy back there has had a turn" and my personal favorite "she's had more hands in her that a catcher's mitt" This was done to establish some heat directly between her and me as opposed to just me and the face wrestler. I even made a point during the match at ringside to continue to taunt her even slapping her ass at one point. The end of the match saw a rather light ref bump to where he was shaking his head trying to clear it out and also looking outside the ring while the heel and the face were recovering in opposite corners. I got into the ring and started to berate the face getting in a couple of cheap kicks while the valet slid into the ring behind me with a frying pan. I insulted the crowd arrogantly then spun around only to find the valet plaster me with the frying pan. I did the Ric Flair classic 2-step then face plant move, she threw her arms up in triumph and the crowd went crazy. She got a few seconds to bask in the glory before the heel recovered and was starting to head towards her. He was cut off in mid-stride by a spear from the face at which point the referee had enough time to recover and quickly do the pinfall count. The heel and I bail out of the ring and the face not only celebrates but acknowledges the valet's blasting of me with the frying pan and the crowd celebrates with the both of them. The frying pan was of course chosen specifically as it does not have a lot of weight, has a large surface area, and makes a loud noise. The angle primarily worked because of the fact that she had not done anything for the previous eight months or so. As a side note to the drama that is professional wrestling, back in the locker room the valet had the biggest grin on her face I've ever seen and she was nothing but enthusiastic in her praise for the idea and how much fun it was. She didn't even ask to do it again and yet her husband couldn't handle that tiny moment of praise that she got and that was the last time she was a valet for us per her husband's "instructions". Insecure and pathetic – hallmarks of far, far too many independent wrestlers.

7. **Being a booker**
Once again, I can safely say I have never encountered a school that teaches anyone to be a booker. I am guessing either it is something they claim you are just born with or, truth be told, they can't train on something they know nothing about. As I pointed out, booking storylines and matches is so far beyond who is going to win and who is going to lose that you need something like this book to even start to understand every aspect that goes into great booking. That might seem like a joke but quite honestly reading

this book from start to finish is probably one of the best educations you can get on how to be a booker so, in effect, this section is the entire book. The key point to take away is that booking is not a simple step 1, step 2, etc., etc. It takes a VAST understanding of psychology, pacing, structure, character, etc., etc. My best comparison is a great booker is like a great fiction author.

8. **Being a Promoter/Owner**
Please note that there is a difference between being a booker and a promoter as far as roles go. Though oftentimes the same person, they do in fact have different tasks and obligations. Again, this is not something taught in wrestling schools. To be fair, it shouldn't be. A degree in business management will be much better suited for being a promoter. The obvious question then is why am I including it in a book about professional wrestling? Not only in my personal observation but in my actual life, the promoter is often times part of the show. As a wrestler, referee, booker, manager, etc. They are also 99% of the time the owner of the company. With all that being said it is important to balance out these different roles to avoid conflict but it also gives you extreme power when you are both and I will relate an example of that later. The biggest issue you will most likely face is your position on the card. The temptation that I have seen more than one owner fall into is that they automatically place themselves in the main event and/or they place some friend, relative, or significant other in the main event or a prominent role. Why this is an issue is that in almost every case the position is neither earned nor is the talent level commiserate with the position on the card. Starting a promotion and putting yourself in the main event on the first card is a recipe for disaster unless you have a proven track record of main eventing shows. Putting a friend, relative, or significant other with 0% experience into that role is even worse, and yet I see this time and time again. This also results in nothing but horrible

morale in your locker room. The litmus test that I use is simple - if there's anyone in the locker room on any given night that can follow the match that you're going to be involved in then they should be in the main event and not you. In order to pass this litmus test however you must be brutally frank and honest with yourself. It may be asking a lot to accept that you are the owner of the business, not just a performer so you must put your ego aside and do what is best for the business not for your ego. If you have a friend, family member, or significant other with almost no experience that hints or even demands to be a part of the show I implore you to test them out in some kind of controlled environment outside of a live crowd. If it doesn't work out, and odds are it won't, you need to have the intestinal fortitude and professionalism to deny them a role in your business if you believe it would be detrimental to the product. If you can't do that then you have no business being in business whatsoever. I myself worked in various roles in my own promotion for over a year before main eventing a show. Remember I said I would relate a story where there is extreme power having both roles? Here's the story of one when I was the owner, booker, and main heel manager having to deal with a situation that sadly is more common than you would think. We had a monthly show at a National Guard Armory for quite some time when the military swapped out the commander of the Armory. This was not uncommon and rarely ever caused any kind of issue. The new commander at this Armory was a little too happy and excited at the fact that there was professional wrestling going on in his building and made a point in our first meeting to express that joy and that he would be attending the first show we had with him as commander. I of course had no issue with this and was excited to have what I thought was an enthusiastic supporter of the promotion. One week after the first show that he attended he requested a meeting with me and at that meeting he rather quickly dispensed with formalities and mentioned that he had a 19-year-old son who dreamed of being a professional wrestler. I told him that was great and a couple of wrestling schools that he might want to look into. Not to be deterred, the commander said he thought it would be a good idea if instead, I put his son on the next wrestling card. I explained that I had a strict policy against using people fresh out of wrestling school much less someone with no experience whatsoever but the commander insisted. It was at this point that the commander just dropped all pretense and said we were not welcome back at his armory unless his son was wrestling on every show. I even tried claiming the insurance would not allow it but there was no convincing him so as a last-ditch effort I said I simply didn't have any wrestler that would be able to work against him as the card was fully booked, I couldn't afford nor find another wrestler to add to the card. The commander said no problem at all as he himself was quite the amateur wrestler in high school and even wrestled in the military so he would be the opponent for his son at no charge. Almost immediately I had the solution so I said that would be great, that I would arrange everything with insurance and for him and his son to show up 30 minutes before the show so we could go over my idea for what was going to happen. On the day of the show, the entire locker room was on edge as they knew that having these two people on the card was going to damage the card quality and they also knew that they would be on every single card going forward. Prior to their arrival I grabbed my main heel wrestler and told him my plan which he was not what you would call comfortable with as he was very scared of ruining everything for everyone but I explained to him that I knew exactly what was going to happen start to finish all he had to do was follow my lead. Both the dad and the son showed up and I laid out my plan for how things were going to go down – as far as they were concerned that is. They were going to be in the opening match of the night and were going to have a few minutes to put on their moves and holds. After those few minutes, my heel wrestler and I would come down to the ring and beat them up a little bit. I told them this will make the crowd absolutely love them. They both enthusiastically agreed and so the show begins and they start to do their ridiculous parody of a professional wrestling match. I didn't give them 30 seconds and then my heel and myself hit the ring carrying kendo sticks. For those not aware a kendo stick is basically a sword-like object made out of bamboo rods that, depending upon how loose or taught they are tied, can be quite painful but not deadly when you strike someone with it. Ours were tied pretty tight and I gave explicit instructions to my heel wrestler that he would take the son, I would take the dad, and neither one of us would be pulling any of the hits at all. I told him to wail into these two with everything you got focusing on the chest and the back as hitting the limbs could cause some damage that would interfere with their day-to-day routines. I'll have to admit my heel wrestler was an insanely nice guy in real life so he wasn't 100% confident in this plan and during the run-in I noticed he wasn't 100% laying in his blows to the son so I made sure to go over and crack on him a few times myself. This was only one half of the plan and it was actually the second half of the plan that I was really focused on. Security helped the father and son to the back while I cut a promo for the crowd to get them back into the show. We then went back to the locker room and the second I was behind the curtain I ran in to the area where the father and son were licking their wounds. Before they even had a chance to speak, as I could see the anger in their eyes, I told them that I hoped they were happy with everything since I instructed my heel wrestler and I myself by extension to take it easy on them during the beat down. I told them that when we wrestlers are in the ring with other wrestlers things are a lot stiffer and more hard-hitting so if we do more then they'll just need to be ready for that. I thanked them for being on the show, then said I had to go coordinate the rest of the show, and walked away before they even had a chance to say anything. Every wrestler witnessing this was shocked but it came as no surprise to me that we were able to use that Armory for many more months and the commander did not even attempt to bring up him or his kid being on our card ever again. The psychology at play is very simple. Like most people who have never actually done something, the commander did not have a real understanding or appreciation for the level of physicality involved in a match. By me telling him the beat down he just received was not as painful as we go through on a nightly basis this was not only cause for concern for him but also put him in a position where his fear of looking weak after taking what he then thought would be a "real" beating was greater than his desire to make his son happy. Additionally, as a protective father, he didn't have any real interest in knowing that his son was going to be hurt on a regular basis. I never brought it up again and neither did he which allowed him to craft the story however he would like and was a tacit acknowledgment that he knew he couldn't push me around. My point in saying all this is that it was me being both promoter and manager that allowed this to occur whereas if I was solely the promoter and had asked a wrestler and manager to do this there is no way that I could ensure the damage I needed to be done was done and that the message was clearly sent nor more importantly that the commander would have gotten the idea that he could not intimidate or bully me, the promoter, personally.

14

Jeremy and I determining who farted!

Mad Man Pondo snorting coke.

2 Tuff Tony powerbombs me through lighttubes on a concrete floor

Pondo and I celebrate despite the fact I am standing there with a freshly torn ACL!

Ian Rotten abusing me for 5 minutes!

Being used as a human weapon!

Handcuffed to the top rope!

Celebrating after slapping Doink!

CHARACTER DEVELOPMENT

(you on steroids - metaphorically)

16

One of the greatest challenges a new wrestler should face is coming up with a good character. I emphasize the word should since it seems these days that most wrestling characters are just "I'm a wrestler". People tend to laugh or scorn at the "old days" when there was a vast, and admittedly mostly terrible, an array of character gimmicks. The plumber, the hockey player, the repo man, etc. are the butt of countless jokes. While those occupations were simple to attach to a wrestler and throw them out to the ring, what many people fail to understand is that psychological character traits that people resonate with should form the foundation for your character. The honorable man, the narcissist, the coward, the overachiever, the cunning, the miserable, and many more. The key is that these are traits that are found within all of us to varying degrees including the negative ones that are put on full display in the ring.

One of the best ways to determine what your character is going to be is to know yourself. More important is to know yourself honestly. If you are honorable then great if you really are narcissistic then accept it and use it as a basis for the following idea - no matter what your character trait is, metaphorically take that trait and put it on steroids for your character. It has been said many times, and it is true, that the best professional wrestling characters are merely an aspect of the real person amplified. The jock in high school good at sports and well-liked by most people needs to take that positive warm attitude and project it out to the whole crowd tenfold. The insecure, angry at the world outcast should funnel that anger into vicious words and actions and direct them towards the crowd. If you have a filter on your behavior in real life that on a scale from 1 to 10 that, for example, is set at 3 then it should be set at 7 in the professional wrestling world. Please note, it is important to never set it to 10. Let's take someone in real life that is a bit of a narcissist, but not annoyingly so, and their friends just say "yeah they're a bit full themselves but that's just so and so". In the wrestling world that person should have no problem letting everyone in the audience and whoever is on the opposing side of the ring know that they think they are the greatest thing going, they have no equal, and that they will win at all cost. A quick note - this behavior should only be in the ring. Wrestlers must have the ability to "turn it off" in the locker room. There is really nothing worse than when a wrestler brings the ring character into the locker room or even worse back home with them. Back to our narcissist, the danger with turning a character trait up to 10 is that it loses all credibility. If it was dialed up to 10 the narcissist would never admit defeat in the match, never get angry at being slighted as they can't even understand that they have been slighted or a myriad of other character traits that are not right for storytelling. There is nothing really more boring than someone who refuses to acknowledge reality. If the match is booked to have a questionable ending the narcissist saying that they won fits in perfectly and is not an issue. If the narcissist is pinned cleanly in the middle of the ring but then in a non-joking manner in every single subsequent interview brings up that they won the match without any storyline reason for them to do so - simply because they thought it was in character - they become a boring uninteresting idiot that the crowd cannot relate to or even dislike as they pity them more than anything.

 I'll go into the physical aspect of your character in a different chapter but it is important here to establish an understanding of how physicality can influence character. Remember that to the audience bigger is better. The smaller wrestler not only should not be bumping left and right for a giant wrestler but it would be foolish for them to craft a character that presented themselves as an unbeatable badass killing machine. It doesn't matter if a 180-pound wrestler was a black belt in three martial arts and a collegiate level wrestler and could easily take down and destroy a 300 pound 6 foot 8-inch clumsy oaf, the audience is only going to see the massive size disparity and believe the bigger person will have no problems with the smaller one. Countless times I have seen technical superiority be transformed into some sort of character trait for the smaller wrestler. Being really good at something is not a character trait. Never giving up despite being a smaller wrestler and having a lower chance of winning, however, is. I have mentioned previously the smaller wrestler Ricky Morton. During interviews, Ricky would acknowledge that the other wrestler was bigger in size but not bigger in heart - great face move as audience members always think they have a big heart as well. He was never boastful and didn't harp on it but didn't shy away from acknowledging that he was on the team that was considered the underdog. This did not damage the character in the least and actually made him, and by extension, his team, even more, appealing to the crowd.

Changing gears, I mentioned earlier that being able to "turn off" and "turn on" your character is essential to the mental health and well-being of you as an individual. There is an ever-present danger, and I've seen it happen far too many times, that perhaps not initially but eventually a wrestling persona will bleed over into the real world for an individual. The main problem I see with this is that it always seems to cause issues with the idea that being a professional wrestler is a job. Like all jobs, it should have a beginning time and end time and there should be a separation between work and home in order to maintain a healthy work/life balance. Too many wrestlers are either "always on" or have such a poorly defined character that it's impossible to tell when they're in or out of character. Every wrestler needs to figure out their own way to keep the two worlds separate. One of the best ways that I found is to view your wrestling gear as a work outfit. You see this in other jobs for example if the work outfit is a suit, overalls, or set of sturdy work boots then you put on the outfit to do the job and you take it off when done. Viewing your wrestling gear like this oftentimes helps create that separation. As a side benefit the more this separation exists, the more you'll be able to foster a unique character inside the ring. There is one other aspect of this that is outside the individual's control. If you craft your character well and it gets over you run the risk of friends or family desiring to interact with the character outside the ring as they simply don't understand that the character is, or at least should be, a job to you. I'll illustrate this with an example from my career. I'd been chugging along for a few years and managed to build up an excellent character that drew heat with the crowd which I combined with an excellent heel wrestler resulted in the two of us being the top draw in the promotion. At this particular point in time, there was a great professional wrestling show every Friday night and I got together with a small group of friends to watch that show every week. One of the guys in the group befriended a rookie manager to our promotion and soon brought him into the fold by watching the show with us. He was extremely green and had not been trained very well but I made sure to treat him with respect and be welcoming as this was a social affair and had nothing to do with my wrestling character - or at least I thought so. Inside the ring on various shows, one of the things that I have become rather adept at was blasting wrestlers with a steel folding chair without hurting them. One week, after the wrestling show on TV, had ended this rookie manager in front of everyone asked me if I could do him a favor. Innocently thinking it was something like giving him a ride home I said sure and then he asked me to blast him over the head with a steel chair. I immediately said "no" and this caused him to begin the begging saying that he thought I was the greatest, I was the reason he got in wrestling, I do it so well, etc., etc. It was, in all honesty, a bit sickening so I cut him off and said "I'm just here to hang out with my friends and watch some wrestling, not to be doing anything like that". He of course didn't accept this and continued on with his begging and pleading even getting a couple of others to join in. Figuring this was never going to end I came up with the best solution I could so I said "okay, fine, just this once". He got really excited, I grabbed the steel folding chair and proceeded to take a full swing stopping an inch from his head and giving it a light tap. I then said "I only blast people in the head when I'm getting paid to do so" threw the chair to the ground and left. He simply did not understand the separation of character and real life.

One of the most difficult parts of having a character is character development. Your character should grow and learn just as we humans do. The character will make mistakes, form alliances, have great triumphs, and suffered tragic losses. The trick is remembering all these things that happened especially if you're working for the same promotion for an extended period of time. The reason is that, like it or not, if you are good at your job and get over with the audience, they will remember all those things about your character in detail and if you act opposite of what they know about you then the willing suspension of disbelief is blown. On the glaringly obvious level, if you are enemies with a wrestler in the past but had no contact for an extended period of time you wouldn't necessarily suddenly be their best friend - the audience would remember "they used to hate each other". Without a sufficient story, it will not make any sense that you're now "magically" friends. In a different example, a more subtle approach that can actually be used to your advantage is if, for example, an angle had been run where an arm was broken two years ago, you could have a new opponent work that same arm giving either the match announcer while calling the match, or you yourself while cutting a promo, the ability to reference the injury. The secret is that as soon as the body part begins to be worked over in the ring those in the crowd will see that as a call back to the injury from a couple of years ago. The golden rule to live by is "the audience never forgets".

If you're in the game long enough, or if you simply change promotions, you will find that you need to have the ability to work either as a face or heel. This is important as far too often I have seen wrestlers that primarily due to a mental block are only able to work one or the other style. The brutal honesty is that the two most common mental blocks that I have found in this area are not mental blocks at all, they're just indications of a bad wrestler. Countless times I have had face wrestlers say they didn't want to be turned heel or work heel in a new promotion because they didn't want the audience to dislike them. The first few times I encountered this I didn't honestly think that they were serious. I quickly realized they were and generally their thought process broke down to one of two issues. Either there is no separation between the person and the wrestler and as such, they felt their treatment in the ring is reflective of them in real life or they took it personally as they didn't understand that being a professional wrestler is a business. These two ideas are often times interchangeable but these are generally the two things I found when probing a little deeper. On the flip side, I often hear from wrestlers that have only been heels that they don't want to be a face because it is boring or it is difficult. If the wrestler finds endearing themselves to a crowd and striving for their acceptance and applause boring or difficult then that says more about them personally than anything else. As for the idea that it is more difficult to be a face than a heel, this is a poor reflection on the ability of the wrestler making such a statement. The implication is either that face wrestlers must be more technically sound and the wrestler refusing to be a face is not or the wrestler is somehow limited in their ability to interact with the crowd. Both concepts are demonstrably incorrect and again reflect poorly on the wrestler making that statement. A solid professional wrestler should be able to work heel or face without any issue and get over in either role.

As the foundation for each role, and for anyone struggling with one role or the other, I present the following big picture concepts to accept, understand and use to build your character in the assigned role. After reading the following do not roll your eyes and say something along the lines of "tell me something I don't already know". Instead, take the statement and start to explore internally what that means to you and how you can apply it to your character. This is the foundation, not the entire structure. Like it or not the foundation must be solid and established for a reason. Having a foundation like this works. Period. It has been tested since the dawn of the sport of professional wrestling. Far, far too often I have encountered wrestlers who downplay this foundation as no longer relevant in an attempt to push their own interpretation or vision of what it should be in "today's world". They fail each and every single time for the simple reason that no one is reinventing the wheel. With all that being said, the foundation for playing the face wrestler is everything must be positive. If playing the heel wrestler then everything must be negative. An additional foundation for the heel wrestler is that you must cheat to be effective. Yes, it is that simple - and of course, at the same time, it is not.

To say that a face is positive is the starting point. You then have to look at your character, as well as other great face wrestlers and determine how you can take that positivity and translate it into something that effectively gets over. Some more broad strokes that can help you with this are as follows: The face is always honest. The face is always honorable. The face always does what is right even if it harms themselves. The face never cheats. The face puts others before themself. The face represents the hopes and dreams of the audience and is what the audience imprints on while engaging in their willing suspension of disbelief. I can't tell you, and there is no secret formula, that if you do this and that and the other thing you will instantly get over with the crowd. You must take the concepts of a face and apply them to your every word and action. You will notice I used the word always when describing some aspects of the face. I want to be clear on this because it is not too difficult for someone to point out a scenario where you should break one of those rules. The face could easily lie to the heel to put them in a situation that is either embarrassing or that ultimately cost them an important match. The point is not that this should never happen but that this should happen so rarely that it actually has value when - and if - it does. All scenarios where a face breaks one of the aforementioned guidelines must be sufficiently crafted to show that the face only did these things after a very large amount of effort not doing them. Everyone in the audience knows that they personally have a breaking point. As they are projecting onto the face so the face is allowed to also have a breaking point. What is most important is that the face breaking point must be beyond the breaking point of the audience member. Since there is no way to know what the breaking point of each and every audience member is the safest course of action is to extend the offense out far more than you think you should. One very basic and simple example is if a heel spits in the face of a face then the face should of course not spit back. The face is supposed to be better than that. There are people in the audience that would probably spit right back in the face of the heel but deep down they would like to think that they are better than that. Others in the crowd would allow it to happen once or possibly twice. The answer however is not necessarily to do something on the third time. The answer is also really not to wait until the 10th time. There comes a point where the audience views the face as weak and a pushover if they allow the offense to go on and on. So how exactly do you know when to pull the trigger? The not only simplest, but best, way and an important lesson for all interactions, is to involve the crowd. After the second spit in the face the face wrestler should grab the microphone and inform the heel that they let them have that but there will not be a third time. The audience is now further drawn in to the conflict as the question of whether the heel is going to push it further - thus causing a confrontation - or walk away thus giving the face a moral victory comes into play. It also allows them to feel like saying that is something they would do as it is a strong dominant position. There are a variety of outcomes from this but I'll display the simplest one to show you how this can be used to further the story of the wrestlers. I've brought this scenario up to a few face wrestlers over the years and the most often reply as to what should happen next is that the heel should spit in their face third a time and the face spits right back in the face of the heel. While it seems logical and is not the worst outcome a slight alteration provides a much greater impact on the audience. The heel spits in the face of the face and then goes on the offense immediately whipping the face off the ropes and executing a back body drop. The heel immediately goes to talk to the crowd while the face no sells the back body drop outside of the view of the heel. The face walks over, taps the heel on the shoulder and the heel disregards him thinking it is the referee. The face does it the second time and the heel brushes it off more vigorously. On the third time, the heel turns around and the face at that point spits in the heel's face opening the possibility for the finisher if that's the planned outcome, or the heel to cowardly roll out of the ring complaining to anyone and everyone that will listen. The added anticipation of when will it happen with the joy of knowing that the face is about to get one up on the heel makes this scenario far more rewarding to that audience than just the quick satisfaction of the single spit.

Face interviews should not only be positive and even borderline uplifting (although not in a cheesy motivational speaker sort of way) but also calm, cool, and collected. There is a time and place for screaming and yelling and that is only when the face has been seriously wronged or robbed by the heel. Screaming, yelling, and being obnoxious are hallmarks of the heel and that is why they should be rarely if ever used by the face. Remember, the audience is imprinted on the face so the cooler the face is, the stronger the connection since everybody wants to be the cool person. Word choice can have a powerful impact on how well you get over. For example, a face can inform a heel that in their next match they are going to beat them up. I am of course using the simplest words and it can be relished up quite a bit but that is the basic concept - the face is going to do something to the heel. Conversely, the face can mention in an interview that the heel is going to regret getting in to the ring with the face. In that scenario, the face is not threatening the heel instead letting the heel know that they are confident that they are better than the heel and that they are more than willing to defend themselves to prove that.

Many rookie wrestlers think that being a heel is easy. They think you just need to come out and scream "F-You" to the crowd and you're instantly a heel. Whereas doing that might make the crowd dislike you, it does not make you a heel wrestler. In fact, it is quite the opposite as everywhere that I've gone I have seen audiences laugh at "heels" that insult them with little else as opposed to actually disliking the heel on a deep level. As wrestling is based in the real world you have to understand that what is generally considered evil in people is not something that they themselves consider evil. Brutal dictators are confident that they are doing the best for their people. Ego maniacs genuinely believe that they are as good as they say they are. To be an effective heel in the professional wrestling world you have to genuinely believe in your words and actions and project things that will be perceived as evil to the audience but not necessarily the character. There is no greater compliment a heel wrestler can receive than getting back to the locker room after a match and having the face tell them that they were convinced the heel wanted to kill them. To be an effective heel you have to commit to your character. The awful horrible things you say to the crowd and/or your opponent must, at that time, be genuine. You don't have to be an Academy award-winning actor or actress to pull this off. A little trick that I find to be effective as prior to going out for the match is to psych yourself up that you're not stepping into the ring with your friend "Bob" but instead with "insert name of Bob's character here". This will make it much easier for your character to completely destroy Bob's character.

An added bonus to being a heel is that it allows the negative character traits that we all have to be set free and put on display. As an introvert, I am not unique in having a general dislike or indifference to other people. This generally manifests itself in me being quiet and non-engaging in social situations. Once the bell rings and I am out in front of a crowd however that means I can finally cut loose, take that dislike, amplify it, don't hold that in, and instead let it out. A big asterisk on this however is there are definitely areas to never cross the line on. Being an unapologetic racist will never get over you and instantly turns off the crowd even if they secretly agree with you. The same thing goes for pedophiles obviously even though I can't imagine anyone building a character around that. Politics are another area to stay away from. Not only for the fact that whether the crowd views you as a face or heel is dependent on their political philosophy thus probably putting you at 50/50 - people merely disagreeing with your political viewpoint is not the basis for an effective heel. I point this out mostly to show that these are not in fact character traits but are often times confused as such. Just as being an introvert is a character trait being narcissistic is a character trait as well. The narcissistic one is easy and fun to play with. If you happen to think that you're the most attractive member of your friend group odds are it's not something that you mention or if you have it is been taken as a sort of joke. Being a narcissistic wrestling heel allows you to not only mention it but mention it regularly and genuinely believe it - or more accurately have your character genuinely believe it. As long as your character trait is a negative one that most people have to one degree or another you can amplify that trait causing the audience to both dislike the fact you have the same negative trait that they do (knowing it is bad) and also a perverse jealousy that you get to let that negative trait free while they can't.

    The other aspect of being a heel wrestler to my never-ending surprise is constantly overlooked is that a heel wrestler must always, always, always cheat! Countless are the times that I have watched wrestling matches where the heel wrestler is so concerned and focused on the next move and hold and how well it's going to be executed that never once do they cheat or if they do it is generally due to a finish that they are required to do. There is a famous wrestler heel quote that goes "when if you can, lose if you must but always cheat". This needs to be enshrined in the eyeballs of anyone who dares call themselves a heel character. I also want to make this very clear that when I say cheat, I mean to cheat. Take the shortcut. Put in the least amount of effort for the most amount of reward. Lie, steal, betray and do anything and everything in the pursuit of your goal. These are some of the core concepts behind the heel that I consistently find lacking. Regardless of their actions, everyone in that crowd considers themselves an honorable hard-working individual. When someone cheats, they reveal themselves to be dishonorable immediately putting them in the polar opposite view of what the audience wishes to aspire to and that is the goal of the heel. The cheating must be with ferocity and quantity. A heel wrestler doing a single eye gauge in a match is not cheating. Doing an eye gauge (or preferably two or three), pulling the trunks, putting the feet on the ropes, and adding in a nice crotch shot for good measure is cheating. There is an additional psychological trick at play here that is often overlooked. The cheating serves to not only prove the individual is dishonorable but that they are unable to engage one-on-one, fair and square, and defeat the face. Consequently, if they cheat frequently, it implies that they are far, far inferior to the face so when the cheating inevitably leads to the loss for the face the anger within the crowd is amplified as they are convinced, possibly even on a subconscious level, that the face is clearly far superior since the heel had cheated so much just to defeat them. Here I must also stress that when cheating the heel must have a look of complete joy or hatred on their face. A blank stare when cheating diminishes the impact of the cheating. Just being a cheater is one thing but taking great pleasure or cheating with malice makes it far more impactful. A simple example of this is the tried and true spot where the heel wrestler drapes the face over the bottom rope facing the crowd and the heel manager comes by to punch or slap the prone face wrestler. I've seen it done a thousand times and probably 995 of those times the slap or the punch was the only thing to occur. I'm using imaginary numbers to drive home the point of course but I had this exact scenario play out more times than I care to count. I mentioned before how I took a simple slap to Doink the Clown and added to it for greater heel energy.

Also, I mentioned before briefly about "tweeners". Not only do they not exist but it is in this context that there are often brought up as an excuse or a "pass" for a face to cheat. As covered before there are very specific scenarios that very rarely will allow a face to cheat so the bottom line is that if you are cheating and cheating well you are a heel. I've seen it far too many times wherein a wrestler will come out, praise the crowd, attempt to get their admiration, and then cheat during the match and genuinely wonder why they can't get over with the crowd.

Explaining to them that their sending conflicting messages completely falls on deaf ears.

For both faces and heels, it is important not only how you say things but what you say. As I previously pointed out the majority of wrestlers I have seen think they are heels by doing nothing more than insulting the crowd using the exact same insults that every single other heel uses and have been using for almost a century – "you suck", "f-you (or fuck you for the classless)", "you're ugly" etc., etc. None of these have any real value in getting over or insulting the crowd. The real value is found in coming up with new ways and different ways to insult people in the crowd that strike at core psychological concepts. An example of how I would approach this is that I would carry around a legal pad in my car and in my office such that when I was not on the road or in the ring and an idea of a way to insult people in the audience came to mind I could write it down. The insults may not even be fully formed and I tried to ensure that they keyed in to some aspect of the average person's psychology that would make them view my character more negatively. Children are an easy and obvious way to do this and yet once again I see little more than "your kids are ugly" or "your kid is a total brat". Sad examples I see far too commonly. I previously recounted an insult towards a mother regarding her infant child and I will put forth a different one here to give you an idea of how this can be executed. I have a stock insult that would be used anywhere in the country and pretty much worked every time. If I found a family, especially with three or more children (more common than you might think), I would single out the parent or parents and indicate that I see their kids and that their kids must be named after what substance they were on when it was conceived so I see your kids are named "Jack Daniels", "Jim Bean" and then I would use other liquor names until there is one kid left (so if there were four kids I would throw in something like "Bud Light") so that always the last kid was named "Mark Meth". The obvious insult for the first few kids is that the parents were drunk during conception, which is bad enough but then insinuating the last one by claiming they were the result of terrible drug abuse the claim really stings. A word of warning here and this insult illustrates it well. When crafting insults and ideas to hurl at the audience you have to make sure you don't become "too smart". Operate on the idea not that your audience is stupid but that they are average. You don't need to dumb it down to avoid the risk of having an insult go over their heads. To illustrate this, I had kicked around eight different final child names for the above-referenced sequence and one of them was "Unknown John". It is not necessarily immediate and visceral but if you think about it for a second there is the implication of prostitution requiring that someone knows that "John" is a slang term for someone who visits a prostitute. It further insults the mother claiming she was a prostitute and she didn't even know who the father was. While that is a decent insult it requires a little bit too much thought to really hit home. On rare occasions, you may find, or accurately feel, that there is a somewhat complicated insult that is too good to let go of. What you can do in this situation is foreshadowing. The parallels between film and television in professional wrestling continue but this is one of the more powerful. Let's say that I really felt the "Unknown John" insult was too good to let go but I agree it would go over quite a few people's heads. A solution, if the opportunity presents itself, would be during an interview earlier on the show (and the more time between these two events the better) claim that I heard that this town was overflowing with prostitutes and that most likely every guy "or as prostitutes call them John's" in this crowd has a "buy 10 get one free" punch card that they regularly fill up. Not a bad little insult but it also establishes the concept of prostitutes and that the prostitutes call people who visit them "Johns". This bit of foreshadowing of the insult to come later in the night also provides the context for it to be impactful so that when I do bust out with the "Unknown John" name people actually know what I'm referring to.

Another mistake I find many face wrestlers engaging in is stating that they are going to defeat a heel or win a match "for the people". This fails on multiple levels. First and foremost, it is a bit presumptuous and possibly even an insult to state that you are going to do something for someone as more often than not they are going to take that as having a little further meaning and that is "because they can't". Despite the fact that the audience member knows they can't run into the ring and beat up the heel they are not necessarily looking for someone to do that for them. However, what they are looking for - and why it fails on a second level - is to be a part of that ass-kicking. The single best way to do this is for the face to always remember and be aware that they are who the audience is projecting on. Ergo, a smart face will present the idea that "with" the support of the fans they will prevail. The use of the word "with" is key as it is now the audience that is part of the ass-kicking through their support as opposed to actual physical involvement. Doing something for someone makes them a passive observer, doing something with someone, even metaphorically, makes them an active participant.

PHYSICAL DEVELOPMENT

(you on steroids - literally)

18

I want to make it very, very clear that this chapter is not here to tell you that you have to go out and pump your body full of steroids potentially damaging yourself for life. What it is going to do is hopefully give you a better understanding of the idea that if you wish to be successful you must understand that wrestlers are larger-than-life characters. This can be accomplished in one of three ways. They can have a larger-than-life personality. This is incredibly difficult and many will argue is something that you are either born with or not and is not necessarily something that can be learned. Think of the individual that lights up a room when they enter or is always and consistently the life of the party. The second way is to be physically larger than the average individual. There is a reason why going back to the birth of professional wrestling wrestlers tended to be above average in height, weight, or musculature. The more above the average often times the more successful they could become. The final way is to have both. These individuals are incredibly rare and easily identified as they are consistently honored as some of the greatest professional wrestlers of all time.

When it comes to physicality the first step is to be honest with yourself. I previously related the story of how I accepted that no audience would realistically believe that someone of my stature would be able to hurt someone of my training buddy's stature. You need to be able to look in the mirror and accept what is reflected back. If you don't see a lot of muscular definition or do see a lot of fat then it is time to make a change. You're going to have to hit the gym but the only way to truly get results is to hit the gym well educated. There is a huge caveat here that

I want to make sure everyone understands that just because you go to the gym and maybe even follow all the instructions here does not mean that you are ever going to possess the size required to pull off being a larger-than-life physical wrestler. I bring this up because the primary thing that I see in professional wrestling rings around the country are either out of shape or in shape but not big enough wrestlers doing a bunch of flip-flop moves and not even beginning to sell properly in the ring. It is universal and it is destroying the credibility of the sport. As difficult as it may be many people must accept that they are simply not physically cut out to be a professional wrestler. I was one of those and it did not prevent me from being involved in the professional wrestling world in the slightest.

You can easily find instructions on different workout routines that emphasize the importance of repetition in the gym, hours of sleep, etc., etc. You will also find some "diet" guides that all seem to be the exact same when you really break them down. It is of course important to eat clean but what none of these diets tell you is that if you're trying to put on size you have to eat a lot – and I mean a lot. When attempting to put on size it is not uncommon to eat 4000, 5000, or even 6000 calories a day. Everyone from bodybuilders to actors to your average hard gainer has used this method to put on size. There are of course two issues with this. For many people, the cost may be an issue. That amount of food could easily run in 2022 dollars upwards of $50 a day. Swapping out meals with protein drinks may reduce cost but will also reduce results. The second issue is far more important. Once you stop eating that much, you will begin to lose size. You may not go back to the same size before you started but you will not be able to maintain the large size without the large eating. I can't recommend enough stabilizing your weight and size before you begin your professional wrestling career.

So where do steroids enter into this? Simply put they can accelerate the timeline for putting on size. It is important to understand however that while the more steroids you take, the faster and larger you will grow, you will also be doing more and more damage to your body. I want to make it extremely clear that steroids are not required in order to put on size. They are a cheat, a shortcut, and a way to possibly damage you for life or even prematurely end your life. With all that said if you are still going to use steroids, you need to be smart about it. The first thing to understand is the prevailing argument amongst steroid abusers that more is better is actually false. You gain X amount of muscle with 50 mg so imagine how much you can gain at 100 mg or 500 mg? This doesn't paint the full picture. Increasing the amount of steroids increases the damage to your body. The following chart provides a great list of potential damage you could do to your body:

Possible Health Consequences of Anabolic Steroid Misuse

Cardiovascular system
- high blood pressure
- blood clots
- heart attacks
- stroke
- artery damage

Hormonal system

Men
- decreased sperm production
- enlarged breasts
- shrinking of the testicles
- male-pattern baldness
- testicular cancer

Women
- voice deepening
- decreased breast size
- coarse skin
- excessive body hair growth
- male-pattern baldness

Infection
- HIV/AIDS
- hepatitis

Liver
- peliosis hepatis
- tumors

Musculoskeletal system
- short stature (if taken by adolescents)
- tendon injury

Psychiatric effects
- aggression
- mania
- delusions

Skin
- severe acne and cysts
- oily scalp and skin
- abscess at injection site
- jaundice

NIDA. 2021, April 12. What are the side effects of anabolic steroid misuse? Retrieved from https://nida.nih.gov/publications/research-reports/steroids-other-appearance-performance-enhancing-drugs-apeds/what-are-side-effects-anabolic-steroid-misuse on 2022, May 10

You are course not going to experience all of these side effects. The point here is that the more steroids you do, the more likely and the greater number/effect of side effects you may experience. So, with all that being said what's the best way to take steroids and avoid as many side effects as possible? The first step is moderation. You can see results from steroid use with as little as 20 mg to 50 mg a day. You do not need to do hundreds or even a gram (1000 mg) to see results. Yes, you will see more results and faster at higher dosages but again, look at the side effects. Realistically speaking I could not conceive of doing more than 100 mg a day. A good test to determine if you're doing too many steroids is if you are taking other drugs to handle the side effects. The inability to sleep is a common side effect of taking high doses of steroids and I've seen wrestlers get prescription sleeping pills because of this. That alone should be enough of a red flag however not only does it not make them change their behavior but another interesting issue arises. One of the side effects of the sleeping pill is diarrhea. So now the bodybuilder is taking a pill to control diarrhea which itself has side effects. Do you see where this is headed? Simply put, it isn't worth it. The second thing you MUST do is cycle when you are using and not using steroids. This will illustrate the point - steroids wreak havoc on your body by flooding it with testosterone. Your body is smarter than you give it credit for and when it notices an abundance of testosterone it shuts down the pituitary gland's production of testosterone as it has what it "needs". If you cycle off steroids the body sees the levels are back below normal and the pituitary gland restarts production. There is however a limit as more than one professional wrestler/bodybuilder will attest, there is a point where production is shut down permanently. Testosterone is so important to so many functions the result of such a catastrophic failure is countless medical issues combined with a lifelong need for testosterone therapy. You can find a variety of recommended cycles but the golden rule to keep in mind is there should be an equal time on as there is off. You will find cycles of six weeks on and six weeks off or even two weeks on two weeks off and I would say that those are probably the safest. Conversely, if it's six weeks on two weeks off you are asking for trouble. Just to clear up any confusion that might exist when I say "on" I am referring to when you are actually taking steroids when I say "off" I am referring to when you're not taking any steroids in any capacity. Another thing you should do while on steroids is eat – a lot. If you're going to be taking the risk, you should see some kind of benefit, and yet countless are the times that overweight or out-of-shape wrestlers have told me they were taking steroids to get in shape when I followed up with what their diet is and how many calories they consume I was consistently met with blank stares or the dismissive "that doesn't matter". Oh, it most definitely matters. Put those steroids to good use by maximizing your workout at the gym and eating a large amount of clean food if you are going to risk your health by taking them in the first place.

So now you have some size from the steroids or smartly just want to be in the best shape possible so you're going to need to cut weight at some point. Contrary to every weight loss pill, plan, and scam that is out there, there is no shortcut. There is an axiom in the bodybuilding world that holds true for everyone: "Abs" are made in the kitchen, not the gym. Even if you continue to work out and possibly take steroids the sixpack is only going to show up when you change up your food choices. You will notice I didn't use the word "diet" as this is not some sort of diet you will go on in order to lose weight or get six-pack abs. Instead, you need to adopt the mindset that moving forward this is simply what you eat. I'm not going to tell you exactly what to eat as nothing needs to be that restrictive. Instead, you need to follow some very simple rules which you must always keep in mind when deciding what to eat. You've seen me use the term "clean" a few times here so what exactly does that mean? Let's start with the simple and most obvious. Foods that have been processed are not clean. This of course begs the question how do I determine if a food is processed or not? The first rule is if it contains ingredients that you either can't pronounce or can't by yourself, it is most likely processed - any idea what on earth Carrageenan is or what aisle I would find it in at the grocery store? The second rule would be if it contains anything to give it color. FD&C Red No. 40, FD&C Blue No. 1, or Tartrazine (a.k.a. Yellow No. 5) to name just a few. Thirdly would be any kind of added sugar or sugar substitute such as Sucralose or Acesulfame Potassium. Lastly would be an abundance of salt. Listed as sodium on the label you should not be getting 50% or more of your daily allowance from one food item. While it should definitely not be eliminated entirely you need to keep your sodium intake as low as possible. The immediate defense that most people throw up is that following those rules eliminates in their mind "all" foods. It of course does not eliminate all foods in many cases merely requires a slight alteration. Instead of buying frozen broccoli in a cheese sauce grab some fresh broccoli which you can then steam or in desperation - microwave. Instead of the breaded frozen chicken fingers grab fresh chicken breasts which you can then cut and prepare into strips yourself with no breading. Hopefully, you get the idea. The stricter that you are with following these food choices the more and the better the results you will see not only in your physique but in your overall health and well-being both physically and mentally. There is science behind that statement and instead of me citing a bunch of works try eating clean for six months and marvel at the difference it makes in your life. I would be remiss if I didn't cover the concept of the "cheat day" or the "cheat meal". While these are real things that could be incorporated into clean eating, I find more often than not they're simply an excuse for bad behavior. If someone suggests going out for ice cream at midnight often times someone will say "sure that would be my cheat meal" ignorant of the fact that ice cream at midnight is going to undo the positive gains of eating clean for the last three days. That being said say you're out with some friends and they decide in the middle of the afternoon to have some ice cream as a nice snack. Getting a single or even preferably child-sized scoop without loading it up with hot fudge, caramel and an assortment of toppings will not undo much of your hard work and still satisfies the desire to engage in a social activity with friends. You have to gauge this yourself as you know if this is the first time you've done something like this in a while or if it is the third afternoon in a row.

There are three other tidbits of information that I'll pass along that will help you on your journey to being in the best shape of your life to assist with your goal of creating a larger-than-life wrestling character. The first is a concept in weightlifting that goes as follows "that which is tracked gets improved". I don't care what method you use - your phone, a piece of paper or in the future a sub-lingual implant - you need to have a workout and you need to track your progress with the goal of incremental improvements. If you are doing the bench press with three sets of eight reps at 180 pounds and you are able to do eight reps on your last set the next time you do the bench press that weight needs to be set to 190 pounds. As soon as you can do eight reps on your last set that gets bumped up to 200 pounds etc. etc. What I have regularly seen are individuals who don't track anything and end up doing that 180 pounds year after year, never improving. Second is a word regarding altering your workout. You will see constant recommendations that you need to change your workout in order to "confuse" your muscles and while there is a certain amount of science behind this at the end of the day the most important thing is consistency. Doing the same workout five days a week every week for a year beats three different workouts each done for two weeks every other month every single time. I would also advise a change in workouts once you hit the 40 to 45-year age range. At that point tendons and ligaments are not as capable of handling very heavy weight so switching to medium weight with perfect form and muscle isolation is the best route to go for continued progress. The last thing is in some respects one of the most overlooked or misunderstood. In order to track your progress and to be satisfied with your results, you need some way to measure. What 99.9% of people use to gauge this is wrong. It does not matter what weight the scale tells you you're at or what percentage a BMI test claims or any other external measurement of some aspect of your body. If you take nothing else from all this workout advice then take the following: the only measure of how well you are doing is the mirror. It doesn't matter how much you weigh or what your BMI is if you don't like what you see in the mirror or if what you see in the mirror is not what you see on the grandest stages of professional wrestling then something needs to change. The mirror does not lie and if you are honest with yourself then you can determine if you are projecting a larger-than-life physique either in size or definition. A word of caution, of course, the mirror is a double-edged sword as it requires you to be honest in your assessment. I can easily find a skinny person who thinks they look fat in the mirror just as I can find a very fat person that thinks they look really good in a mirror. You have the template for what great professional wrestlers look like. If you're not seeing that in the mirror it's time to make some changes.

It is been said many times before and will forever remain true - there are no shortcuts on the road to success. Taking steroids may seem a good way to accelerate much faster down that road but as I pointed out, it can come with a rather steep price tag. If you're going to use steroids, I certainly won't judge you but pay attention and follow the safety recommendations I've listed here to ensure not just a long career in professional wrestling but a minimization of the long-term detrimental health effects as ideally you would want a healthy life after your wrestling career is over. A quick search will find countless articles and stories of not just professional wrestlers but many a professional athlete whose life after retirement was a living hell due to the dangerous effects of steroid use.

19

STRUCTURING A MATCH

(by not planning out every move)

20

Where I have seen much of what is wrong with professional wrestling today is in how poorly the matches are constructed. When watching wrestlers in the locker room structuring their match, I tend to see two different methods - both of which are wrong. The first method, which is not the most used method but nonetheless very prevalent, is to plan out nearly every single move, hold, counter move, and counter hold. It goes something along this line "we'll lock up, I'll whip you to the ropes, come off with a clothesline, then I'll drop the leg, then I'll pick you up and whip you into the corner, I will give you a spear then a second spear then straddle the ropes and give you the 10 count punch. On the 10th punch, stand up with me on your shoulders and do a powerbomb" etc., etc. They will then proceed to layout move by move every single thing that is going to happen in the rest of the match. They don't necessarily memorize every single sequence (though I've seen that too!) in its entirety but they use this to plan out large chunks of the match and if there is an issue - which of course there always is - they can come back to it by jumping to a different section rather easily. The second and more common method is a broad outline such as "okay will start the match with me up and I'll get some shit in, then you reverse it and get your shit in, then I'll reverse it and set you up for the big (insert "signature" move name here) but you block it then hit me with a big powerbomb and be up for a little while then I'll eventually reverse it and get my shit in" etc., etc. until the finish. Both these methods fail and fail for the same reasons.

First and by far the most important is that nowhere in any of that planning is the acknowledgment of a crowd. The entire focus is on the wrestlers and what they will do either specifically or in broad terms. It is about their moves and their holds and not about the paying audience. A perfect illustration of how bad this can be is seen when you look at how a great professional wrestler structures a match. The conversation will start something like this: "Okay, we will start with you getting your heat on me". Notice there's not a single reference to any move or hold whatsoever. The only concern is getting heat which specifically references the crowd. The goal is to get a reaction from the crowd and this is accomplished through moves and holds. The next thing modern wrestlers often say to me is "okay that's great you have to acknowledge the crowd but you still have to know what moves to do, so you have to plan out the moves". The answer to that is yet again a reference to the amazing wrestlers of the past when asked about what moves and holds will they plan to do prior to their match starting always answer with a simple "we'll call it in the ring". There is a lot of course to that statement beyond just the surface so let's break it down.

Great wrestlers understand that what moves and holds you do is almost completely irrelevant. The more elaborate, complex, or acrobatic the move the more likely it is to result in injury and the less impactful it is to the crowd unless it is used only once in a match. What truly matters is that whatever moves you choose should be structured in a way that engages the crowd and tells the story not only of the current angle you're involved in but the story of the match as well. In very broad strokes it is important to keep in mind that the heel should be up for most of the match and cheating as often as possible. This is why generally speaking the heel calls the match in the ring. Working with the referee and possibly a manager they can ascertain how well things are getting over with the crowd and adjust accordingly. It might be time for a fake comeback from the face or more interaction might be required in order to further engage the crowd from the heel are a couple of examples. Wrestlers have a wide array of tools in order to manipulate a crowd and these should be structured into the match. I've covered some of them for that you that might be familiar with such things as:

- The face takes immediate control of the heel consistently embarrassing them with the face's superior skills until the heel cheats to take over control.
- The heel consistently refuses to engage the face by bailing outside the ring every time it looks like the face is going to get in offense
- Particularly effective with tag teams - the face team consistently getting the heel team to mess up their attempts at double teaming and as a side effect getting them to accidentally hit each other
- The heel manager distracts the referee at just the right moment allowing the heel to cheat and take over on the face or avoid a clear pinfall

The list goes on and on and there really is an infinite number of things to do to engage the crowd. The important thing to note here, and what I have had several people ask me about or claim is "missing", is that nowhere in here are wrestling moves and holds such as body slams and power bombs. Those things can be a part of the structuring of the match but the goal here is to create a mindset that the true structure of a match is not specific moves and holds but what story is to be told and how to engage the audience in that story. A quick note about the short list of things you can do above. When running these by wrestlers I sometimes hear things like "that is silly", "that is stupid" or the classically dismissive "that's old school". This tells me right away that I'm not dealing with a quality professional wrestler as even if I were to accept those opinions as being valid (which I don't) the actions on that list are also one other thing – "things that work in getting over with the crowd". This is why insulting them speaks poorly of the wrestler that does this and exposes them as someone that doesn't understand that they are there to wrestle for the crowd and not for themselves.

Very good wrestlers are also keenly aware of time. At a certain level, especially if your match is to be televised, you will be required to maintain a time limit. Well-seasoned wrestlers will be able to adjust the structure of the match based on how much or how little time they have to complete the match. Delay tactics and rest holds have no place in a three-minute burner. Conversely, you don't want to do a flurry of 10 consecutive moves in the opening minutes of a 30-minute match. It is not merely a question of a wrestler blowing up during longer matches or not having enough time to rest. There is a pace to matches that needs to be built up from start to finish in parallel with the time limit given to the match. Sadly, this is a skill that pretty much can only be picked up with practice. This is one of the other things that I have never seen any training school provide - repetitive training on timed matches. There should be ample opportunity to get into a ring at a training school and do a four-minute match. Have an instructor evaluate the pacing and/or structure and then do the four-minute match again. Repeating as many times as you can as there is no "getting it right". It is more to gain an appreciation for structuring a match under that timeframe with the obvious implication that the same training could occur for 10-minute matches, 30-minute matches, etc., etc.

Many wrestlers will correctly point out to me that there is one part of the match that must always be planned out and discussed in advance and that is of course the finish. Here again, it is a matter of focus. It is nothing at all to find wrestlers planning a finish where there is little more than "you reverse that, hit your big move, and then pin me". If there is no planned angle for after that then their discussion generally ends. What I should be hearing is something more along the lines of "reverse that move but then pause and get your heat, then hit your big move for the finish. Get your heat with the crowd while I am arguing with the ref to get my heat then I'll make a move like I'm coming at you, then you stance up like we're going to fight then I'll bail and head back to the locker room while you get your heat." As always, I must point out that in the second scenario the focus is on interacting with the crowd. Yes, the moves in sequence of events to achieve the finish are covered but they are not the focus. The focus is and always should be on how the moves will allow the wrestlers to interact with the fans and in specific regard to the finisher how the moves and interacting with fans moves along the storyline.

21

HOW TO BOOK A STORY

(just ask one question)

22

Not just for bookers, this section can be insanely valuable to everyone involved in the wrestling product – managers, referees, performers, etc. To start let's take this all-too-common booking story I often see on the independent circuit. With little variation it tends to go something like this "okay, you guys have a match and then the heel wins. We'll have a few rematches without a clear victory by the face then will have this final blowout match and playing wrestling 'whack-a-match' it looks like it will be a no disqualification falls count anywhere match". On paper, it looks relatively harmless but as far as the crowd is concerned it is boring as hell. So, the question obviously becomes how do you make it not boring? The answer is simple and it ties into the one question to ask always and in every step of the story – "why?" The "why" behind the action is what will engage your audience or send them heading to the restroom for a break waiting for something more interesting to come along. In many respects, the "why" is really the only thing the audience is interested in. It's the story, it's the soap opera and if you don't understand the proper application of the question then you'll never create or take part in a compelling story. It is the one question you need to ask to competently book a story.

The why is not only key and essential but also allows you to flesh out and create an even greater detailed story which assists in engaging the crowd. Let's take the first component of that basic booking idea and ask ourselves why the two (or more) wrestlers are having a match? Operating on the idea that this is the beginning of the story some people might say "well there isn't really any reason why, they just were put together to start the story". There is really nothing more boring for the crowd than for there being random people in the ring for no apparent reason. If this is the start of a feud then before the bell rings to start a match the heel should be on the microphone insulting or laying out a motivation for why this match is happening. Here are a couple of quick and simple ones: the heel could state that they are going to obtain a certain belt or goal and the heel is the first stop on their way to that goal with the face ultimately winning the match and so the heel is now going to focus on revenge against the face for the loss or it could be that the heel goes on and on about how attractive and popular the face is with other wrestlers and members of the opposite and/or same-sex so they're going to make sure by the end of this match the face has been made so ugly they will lose that ability/attraction, etc. Not only does the audience now have why they are fighting, and thus some interest in the outcome, but the mere act of asking "why" opens up an infinite number of possibilities. Take for example the scenario where the heel wants to ugly up the face out of jealousy. If at the end of the match the heel has the face completely at their mercy and then proceeds to do something to attempt to damage their face what stops them from fulfilling their stated goal? If you just have a match where the heel says they will make the face ugly and then proceeds to do so, the story ends. Instead, you see how several attempts must be made, they must fail so now you have to figure out WHY it fails. Did the referee interfere at the last minute? Was it a commissioner or figurehead? What about a friend of the face coming down for the save? You begin to see quickly how booking ideas flow seamlessly when you start to ask why things are happening. Continuing on with the story we set up, there would be a rematch between these wrestlers that you have to ask yourself a question the audience will be asking - why would the heel accept a rematch? If the heel loss prevented them from achieving a goal but they would have a chance at gaining it during a rematch which would provide a "why" for the heel to accept a rematch. If that is missing however things become a bit more complicated. A win/loss record is meaningless to a heel so getting revenge against the loss in and of itself is not a valid why. If the heel was successful in at least partially injuring the face someone might be tempted to say that the heel accepting a rematch "why" is because he wants to finish damaging the face but that flies in the face (so to speak) of what makes up part of any heel persona which is that they are basically cowards. It should be made apparent to the audience that the heel knows the face is superior to them so they will not engage when things are fair. Heels always cheat, always seek a shortcut, and always seek the least amount of pain or inconvenience to themselves. A couple of basic ways to get a rematch would be: the face interferes in a match that the heel is having with a different face denying the heel the victory in that match angering them to the point where they accept a rematch in order to punish the face or they accept the rematch on the condition that the face does some random act such as putting a belt on the line (if applicable), or arranging a date with the faces valet, etc., etc. Once again, the point in this is trying to illustrate that at every step you must ask the question "why?" and have a logical, common sense answer the audience understands and can relate to.

When dealing with wrestlers at a high level having a "why" on their match allows them to elevate it even more. Following through on our current storyline if the end of the match sees the heel beating on the face of the face in an attempt to make them ugly high-level wrestlers would remove all punches to the face from their match. They would understand that in order for something to have the highest impact (pun intended) it needs to be something out of the ordinary within the context it's presented. So, if the face is being punched in the face at various times in the match it doesn't really mean a lot when they get punched a lot in the face at the end. Conversely, and this operates on a subconscious level if the audience hasn't seen a single punch to the face the impact is heightened when all the sudden it is the sole focus. To give you an idea of how important it is when I was running my own promotion, I would gather all the wrestlers together as soon as everyone arrived in the locker room and informed them of what was going to be considered major moves involved with angles over the course of the evening so that they knew what to avoid in their matches. If there was going to be a chair shot causing a disqualification or something to that effect no chair shots were allowed that night. If a piledriver behind the back of the referee was going to change the tide of the match instantly no one was allowed to do piledriver the entire night, etc., etc. those edicts were obviously on a large scale but as I just pointed out having a "why" allows a wrestler to make changes on a smaller scale such as the things that go on in their match.

    I shouldn't have to say this but I see it time and time again. Booking a story should never take place match to match. There should be a pre-planned beginning, middle, and end transition. I'll explain the end transition later but for now, let's take a look at the basic story outline we started with. The blow-off of that is a no disqualification, falls count anywhere match. From what I've seen most of the time this is done just because a promoter or wrestler thinks it would be cool or fun or it's just how you end a feud. They are of course wrong on all counts and something truly interesting happens when you ask "why" are they having a falls count anywhere no disqualification match? There has to be a reason and the reason can be very simple. For example, over the course of the various matches between the face and heel has there been more than one disqualification finish to a match? Disqualification finishes are frustrating to the crowd by design as they don't illustrate a clear victor. Having a no disqualification match not only eliminates any doubt in the mind of the audience that there will be a winner (which of course you can cleverly book around but that's a different story) but also that they can expect a higher level of violence as neither the face nor the heel has to worry about being disqualified for engaging in illegal moves or activities (though the face continues to refrain from cheating). The falls count anywhere aspect is a shade more difficult but not too terribly. I ran this type of match as an end transition between two wrestlers but I made sure in the match right before this match that the heel very clearly pinned the face on the floor outside the ring with the referee in the ring screaming that the fall only counts inside the ring. This allowed the heel to cut a promo saying they were the one who desired the falls count anywhere since they had already proved to the face and everyone in the crowd that they can beat the face and they don't want to lose out on a technicality because it wasn't in the ring. The key point here is that knowing the "why" of the ending of the match or the type of the match, in this case, can not only directly influence but also help out the booking of the matches prior to it as well as increasing the interest of the crowd not just in the match but in the entire story (which is of course far more important).

Continuing our filmmaking analogy, I need to point out the fact is it is important to show the "why" instead of telling the "why". A perfect example is what I just referenced above whereby the heel pinned the face very clearly outside the ring. There could just as easily have been a scenario whereby a heel could, in an interview, claim that they could beat the face outside the ring but it would hold no real weight and would not add to the stakes as it is not yet been shown to be a possibility. Another glaring example would be if the heel suddenly becomes romantically interested in a face's valet. Yes, they could do an interview explaining how attractive they find the valet or how the valet would be so much happier with the heel rather than the face, etc., etc. and it would be more effective if prior to that the heel had made a point to invade the personal space of the valet or offer them some token of affection or generally make it very clear physically in person that they were interested. There is also an aspect of showing that has to do with how a wrestler acts in the ring but ties indirectly with booking and storylines and has everything to do with showing instead of telling. Sadly, I've also noticed that this seems to be one of the most overlooked and/or poorly executed aspects of a professional wrestling match. Simply put, wrestlers must show conviction behind their words and actions. A heel in a feud with a face must convey to the audience their utter disdain and hatred for their opponent. They should be able to see it in the face of the heel while they're beating on the face. The attacks must be vicious and unrelenting to such a level that the crowd feels sorry for the face (remember they are imprinting on the face so you're effectively beating them down as well and the more they feel beaten down the greater their joy when the tables are turned). As a face, you must be able to show that that beating is truly vicious, is doing damage, and may even knock you down for the count. In different booking, you need to be able to show on your face that you've reached a point where you're not going to take it anymore, you're going to rise up and overcome this adversity. I know I said it before but I am going to harp on it again because it is an epidemic - I do not see this on the faces of most wrestlers in the ring and instead, I see them waiting their turn to be "up" or hyper-focused on executing some silly flip-flop move. The truly sad part is that you don't even need to be good at conveying the ideas I just listed. Remember, people are walking in to the building with a willing suspension of disbelief. They are already halfway there to buying into the idea that this heel really hates this face. Lean into that just a little and the match will be enjoyable for the crowd, lean in to it a lot, and you and have a superstar in the making. The belief is fragile however so you must make sure to maintain it. This story might illustrate what I'm talking about. There was a local promotion close to where I lived that really wasn't very good. I would go a couple of times a year just because it was close or because I knew a wrestler that was sort of slumming it with them as they had nothing else to do that weekend. They had a manager who was a relative of the promoter that was suffering from some degenerative condition that required him to use metal poles to assist in walking and also distorted his physical appearance. He was a face manager (so now you know the level of promotion I was dealing with) and I caught wind through the grapevine that they were bringing in a heel manager who would be attacking this face manager in order to get instant (and most likely cheap) heat. When the event finally unfolded the heel manager said quite a lot of things (poorly) on the microphone and then kicked one of the walking poles out from this face manager's grip resulting in them collapsing to one knee and then the heel manager shoved the face manager to the mat. At that moment the willing suspension of disbelief was blown. It was very apparent to everyone in the crowd that they were "taking it easy" on this face manager due to his affliction. If the affliction is such that the individual is not able to perform when needed then they should not be part of the show in any way, shape, or form. Wrestling is a for-profit business, not a charity and as cold-blooded as you think that might sound the fact remains true. All is not lost however as after the show I ran into the wrestlers at a bar and I went over to the face wrestler and acknowledge that he had sold the angle rather well (which he had in all honesty) and I asked him if he was the one who told the promotion to only do the one pole kick and the shove as he physically couldn't handle anything beyond that. He said no not at all that he in fact had told them he was fine and up for just about anything and even had a wrestler helping him learn how to do some bumping behind the promotion's back. I've encountered this a few different times where people are so overly sensitive and fearful that they underestimate others and as they're not willing to take any chances, everyone suffers. This promotion was so scared of hurting the guy they wound up hurting their own show. I asked if he was able to stand at all on one crutch and he said sure no problem but he thought it looked better to collapse when one had been kicked out from under him. I left things at that but through the wrestler, I knew there I found out that the angle had absolutely no heat whatsoever and died within two shows. I was not surprised in the least bit. About a year later, partially because my friend was still there and partially because the promotion was starting to gain a little traction and even attracted a couple of other good wrestlers, I wanted to try something out as I thought it would be fun so I convinced the promoter to let me come on as a heel manager for my friend and have free reign with my booking which he agreed to because he had been familiar with the promotion that I owned and the successful creative booking that went on there. On my first night there, I set up a post-match run-in with my guy after a match with the guy who had the face manager with the crutches. Before the match, I pulled both of them as well as their opponent in that match aside and informed them of what was going to go down in explicit detail. I don't think I ever saw such a large smile on anyone's face as the guy with the crutches so I knew things were going to work out well. The match went down as planned and shortly after the faces were celebrating their victory me and my heel wrestler ran to the ring. I grabbed the guy with the crutches who was outside the ring (by design) and allowed my heel wrestler to viciously attack the face wrestler quickly executing a big move so that the face would have to sell for some time. This was done so that what I was about to do would not distract from the actions in the ring. Once the face was down and selling, I dragged the guy with the crutches over to the announcer's table and proceeded to slam his head into the table repeatedly causing a mess and moving down the table a foot at a time (slamming his head each time) then moving on to the guardrail smashing his head again and again. At this point, the crutches were gone and between my holding him up by his hair and his own ability to semi-stand without the crutches it all came off beautifully. I finally rolled him into the ring and pointed at my heel wrestler who then picked up the face manager, climbed to the top rope, and executed a super bomb off the top rope. We had prepped and practiced with the kid earlier in the day making sure that he knew how to take the bump and also having confidence that because I had trained my wrestler properly, he knew how to protect the kid during the move as well. I then proceeded to take the mic and inform the crowd of who I was and that I beat the holy hell out of the face manager with the crutches because he was weak and I didn't like the way he looked. The crowd was visibly shocked and shaken that such vicious beating had been dished out on what they perceived to be a "handicap" individual. It worked perfectly. When we got to the back face manager with the crutches could not express enough how grateful and excited he was to finally be doing something instead of just walking around the ring as a cheerleader. I informed them we were far from over as the real treat will come midway through the feud. It was during that mid-feud match that the face had won by disqualification where my plan continued. The face got a really big move on the heel which he would have to sell for quite some time and then through a preplanned placement of myself in the ring, I was cornered and could not escape. The face gave me a powerbomb which, being a small manager, would knock me out of any kind of retaliation for some time and then put me upside down in the ropes so that my crotch area was exposed near the top turnbuckle and my head was almost on the mat. He called the face manager with the crutches into the ring and per my instructions prior to the match the face manager raised one of the crutches into the air which elicited a great reaction from the crowd and then slowly rotated and lowered the crutch to point to my crotch. The crowd went absolutely nuts and while the face wrestler held him up the manager dropped one of his crutches and then with both arms proceeded to take the other crutch and smash it into my crotch not once, not twice, but repeatedly many times. After about 10 times the face manager raised the crutch in his hand in celebration and again the crowd went absolutely crazy. Then, with the face wrestlers' help, they both got out of the ring and made their way up the ramp with one last celebratory crutch raise to the crowd which of course was met with a deafening roar. Following one of the three rules - protect yourself - I was wearing a metal cup which, considering the non-expert level of the blows inflicted by the face manager, saved my sex life. Nonetheless, the entire angle got over since the initial beating was so vicious and beyond what the crowd was expecting that the heat was instantaneous, intense, and most importantly, real. The revenge needed to be equally as vicious and intense and nothing beats a good crotch beating to get a point across. Furthermore, as it was manager-on-manager violence, it did not affect the desire in the crowd to see the face wrestler finally get over on the heel wrestler. Every part of the angle was planned not just to get the story moving along but also to ensure that none of the actions break the willing suspension of disbelief. There are quite a few different ways I could have beat up the face manager initially but I purposely chose one where I was damaging his head and not his arms or legs as the perception from the crowd is that those were weak and non-functioning. The side benefit of course is that I could hold him and control him by the hair and I also have the knowledge that he himself said he could stand without the crutches. You'll also note that post-match beat down outside the ring consisted of a single move inside the ring. The willing suspension of disbelief would once again be broken if the big giant wrestler continued to execute move after move after move on the defenseless, "handicapped" individual. Think of the one move as an exclamation point! The viciousness of the attack also provides the perfect answer to the question "why". The face wrestler now has an insanely strong revenge motivation to go after the heels. As to "why" me and my heel would accept follow-up matches, the reasons were of course provided to the crowd for each match but that's not important to go into here.

There is a counterpart to asking "why" that sometimes goes overlooked so I would be remiss if I didn't mention it here. When booking you may find it sometimes prudent to ask yourself the question "why not"? Countless times I've been in booking meetings where an idea would be presented and no good answer as to why a certain wrestler would do that presents itself so flipping around and asking why they would not do that is often a good way to either flesh out an idea or spin it off in an entirely different direction. Take the above scenario with the "handicap" manager and me. While booking the logical question came up why would I attack the face manager again? An infinite number of answers to that question presents itself however when you switch it around to "why wouldn't I attack the face manager again" you begin to understand that each subsequent attack diminishes the impact of the first. It also opens up the idea that perhaps I regularly make an attempt to attack the face manager but it is always booked in such a way that I'm prevented by the face wrestler or other outside forces from getting my hands on that face manager. This then leads to the possibility of a motivation to agree to a match whereby if my wrestler wins, I get five minutes alone with the face manager. The twist on the classic wrestling angle of the face wrestler getting five minutes with the heel manager but again by simply asking the question "why not" we potentially open up an entirely new direction for the angle or at least part of it. Asking this question can also ensure that you don't overlook anything. Constantly focusing on why someone is great but peppering in an occasional well why wouldn't they do this you often find that there is actually no reason that they would not do something, therefore, they should do something and thus new opportunities present themselves.

We now move on to one of the more advanced, difficult, and rarely seen storyline concepts in modern professional wrestling – layering. Layering is nothing more than the word I've used to describe this. Easily go into a thousand wrestling locker rooms speak to a thousand bookers and they will tell you they have never heard the word layering so don't get hung up on that. What I mean to say is that your storylines should have two components that I will call layering.

The first is that the storyline between two wrestlers or two tag teams should not be an island unto itself. If every single card for six months or a year it's the same two wrestlers wrestling each other it quickly becomes stale and repetitive. They need to face other opponents and that is where things get very interesting and fun and admittedly difficult for those truly interested in storytelling. The reason is that now, when crafting a storyline, the booker will have to not only take into consideration the storyline of the other wrestler but how those two storylines could possibly clash, interact with each other, or need to be put on the shelf for that match in order to move both stories along. In its simplest and most obvious form let's say the heel was having a match against an up-and-coming wrestler with no real stakes involved and they were taking it very seriously as the newer wrestler was clearly outclassed. The cliché that does work is at some point the face wrestler is involved in a feud with the heel wrestler comes down executes a move on the heel behind the referee's back and allows the up-and-coming wrestler to pin the heel. Simple but effective.

The second and oftentimes even more challenging concept is that no feud should end without a new feud for the parties involved to be started or already ongoing (with the obvious exception of a wrestler leaving the promotion). I hope I don't need to remind you this is a male soap opera we are creating here. Things in real life don't just simply start and stop with very clearly defined beginnings and ends. There is an ebb and flow to the way our lives go. This should be mirrored in the storylines of the wrestlers. As long as you have a valid "why" it can oftentimes be far simpler to move into a new feud based on past experience than creating the feud from scratch so to speak. On a very simple and basic level take for example the story where in the middle of a feud between two wrestlers, the face wrestler has a match with an unaffiliated heel and in the course of that match the heel involved in the feud with the face attempts a big move on the face but misses and hits the other heel opponent in the ring which the face then capitalizes on and pins the heel in the ring that he has the match with. The final blowout match the face and the heel that have the existing feud going on ends with the heel being helped to the back and the faces celebrating inside the ring. After a short amount of celebration, the heel that was pinned in the aforementioned match runs down to the ring attacking the face from behind and beating the holy hell out of them. This not only fulfills the requirement of having a face get beat up every time after they win a big match and also allows this new heel to cut a promo in the ring claiming that this face and their ridiculous argument with the other heel cost this heel a loss and they were now going to take revenge. This has the nice bonus of really good heel psychology as the other heel really cost them the match but they projected the loss on to the face without any justification. Many will be quick to point out that this satisfies the new feud for only half of the equation as what is the heel to do now and that is why I said this is one of the more tricky aspects of booking. You need to have multiple stories going and have multiple wrestlers cross-pollinating storylines. Like anything else in life, the greater number of variables the greater the complexity. The secret is to find out what level of complexity you're comfortable with as a booker. We can't all be Eddie Graham, Bill Watts, or Jim Cornette, but we have to have the ability to juggle more than one storyline and involve more than two or four wrestlers. What you will find invariably happens is that you will have a good storyline for some wrestler to get involved with a non-feud wrestler and that the actions or activities conflict with the storyline that the first wrestler has going on. The trick that I found works and has worked since the dawn of wrestling is to take detours and side routes but always return to the main road. Using another basic and simple example let's say you have two pairs of wrestlers with their own storylines going on so 2 faces and 2 heels. You do a match where a face and heel go against each other as non-feud opponents. Some good booking in that match would result in some controversy and intrigue ultimately leading to a tag team match between the 2 faces against the 2 heels. This could easily be overbooked or even set up a small string of matches but for our purposes, it would be a simple one-off and would represent a side road that was taken on each one of the feuds but then they returned to their main route and didn't have anymore tag team matches of this sort. I'm obviously giving you very simple and broad strokes of how to have inter-connected booking but when done properly this not only engages the audience to a greater degree but ensures that they keep coming back for more and more.

The concept of the booking committee is a mixed bag these days so want to make sure that you understand a booking committee can be invaluable only under specific conditions. There are two specific conditions that must be met for a booking committee to work. The first is that the individuals involved must mentally be adults, be open-minded, and have an understanding of the booking concepts discussed in this book. That may sound very simple and obvious but from my experience, it's not. Understanding booking concepts is difficult in and of itself but then requiring that someone be open-minded, mature, willing to compromise, and willing to work well with others is a tall order. From what I've seen booking committees are often plagued by friends, relatives, the top drawing wrestler, or other parties that generally are only on the committee due to their relationship to the promoter/booker. I've brought it up before this is a business and when selecting who is on the booking committee personal feelings and attachments cannot be deciding factors unless of course the individuals are eminently qualified at which point the relationship status should not matter. The second condition is that there must be someone in charge with final say capabilities that is strong enough to stand by their decisions. There is no way that you are going to get everyone to agree on everything so there must be someone who is able to accept one idea, dismiss another, and not be swayed by the arguments for or against either. While not a dictator, a true head of the booking committee will be able to listen and elicit feedback from the others, and if the consensus can be reached great but if not they need to be able to say the direction that they will be going in and that will be accepted without argument. This is yet another reason that personal connections are often times, not the best since telling a relative or significant other that their idea is not going to be used can often times spill over into the personal life yet it may be the right decision for the promotion. I would also caution against having any wrestler on a booking committee. It has nothing to do with their intelligence or booking knowledge and everything to do with the perception of favoritism. If they are not an active wrestler then you could probably get away with it right up until the point that they become involved in the wrestling product at which point in time I can't stress enough they should be removed from the booking committee. Remember it is not personal it is business.

BOOKING SUPPLEMENTAL – HOW TO BOOK A SHOW

Since we are talking about booking, and even though this chapter is technically about a story, I need to touch on the idea of how to book a show. From what I've seen these days the booking consists of little more than "the main event is the last match on the show". When setting up a wrestling show you have to make a conscious decision of where every single match on that show is going to occur. In its simplest terms and using a house show with six matches as an example you want to apply the "roller coaster" philosophy. Stripped down to its most basic elements a roller coaster ride will have buildups with payoffs that continue to escalate until the big build-up and big payoff at the end. The following plan is specific to the six-match card: the first two matches of the night would build to a nice payoff in the third prior to an intermission. The interest level of the crowd will wane during the intermission so the next two matches after the intermission should be even bigger builds than the two earlier in the night with the main event being the final huge payoff. This is of course not set in stone as I've used the opening match of the card to be huge and impactful with the next two matches leading down to an almost disappointing intermission and then grabbing their interest after intermission on a sort of high then drop low for the fifth match and then go home big with the finale. A lot of what influences your match layout is the storylines that you have going but what you want to mostly take away from the two examples I've given you is that there needs to be, from the audience's perspective, highs and lows. A well-planned out wrestling card should be an emotional roller coaster.

Another aspect of planning out the match order will have to do with the level and quality of talent in your locker room. This can impact you in three important ways. If you don't have a strong locker room with consistent quality across the board or, if for some external reason you're forced to utilize a less talented wrestler, your best option is to "hide" them on the card. The best hiding place is the second match of the night. The opening match needs to be something to immediately hook the crowd and focus their attention. The next match should certainly build if it can but if you have to hide someone this is the place to do it as you still have the rest of the card to pull the crowd back in. The very first wrestling promotion that I ran I did so with three other individuals. Two of them were wrestlers one quite good and the other quite bad. Since the quite bad wrestler was technically an owner of the company and had an oversized ego, they demanded that they be wrestling on every show. It became very evident very quickly that myself and the other non-wrestler had all the booking ideas and consequently the booking was left to us and we quickly moved to "hide" the bad wrestler/owner in the second match of every card. The next way that it can impact you is that you have to be aware of who puts on the best match in your locker room - by that of course I mean the wrestler(s) who are most engaged by the crowd - and ensure that you write proper storylines to suit them and they have proper placement on the card. I've seen it happen in many promotions and, admittedly, have been at the center of the issue on more than one occasion personally where the owner of the promotion has a prominent position on the card. I mentioned before that I and the wrestlers that I manage over the years almost universally adopted the philosophy that we were going to go out and put on such an amazing match and engage the audience so much that no wrestler would be able to follow us. On more than one occasion I have found myself (or witnessed other talents in a different promotion) in a position where we, the superior talent, were placed lower on the card and it did irreparable harm to everything that came after it. I could care less how arrogant that sounds as it is a simple fact. If you have someone out for the second, third, or fourth match that has the crowd frothing at the mouth angry or sad or ecstatic or whatever emotion that you are attempting to elicit from them and no match on the card after that is able to reach the same level each subsequent match provides a diminishing return as the audience will become less and less engaged and more and more disappointed. The only thing worse that a booker can do - that I have witnessed on many, many occasions and again been party to myself personally - is when the superior talent is put on right before the "main" event. It doesn't matter if the main event is a title match with a wrestler who is the booker of the promotion or a visiting "celebrity" wrestler, their match will be rendered moot and pointless if it is blown away by the match right before it. Not only the best, but honestly the only, course of action is to put the highest quality wrestlers you have in the main event of every card unless booking dictates otherwise. To give you an extreme example of how great booking can make this work I was faced with a booking dream come true. On the same card, I was going to have the very first-ever meeting between the wrestler I was managing, Mad Man Pondo, and the legendary Abdullah the Butcher. Depending upon what year it is when you read this book, those names may not mean anything to you but in the realm of hardcore wrestling at the time that match was considered a dream match between an established legend and a possible future legend. As a testament to this, we had people coming from as far as a thousand miles away just to see this match. On the same card, there was to be a title match between my wrestling counterpart Jeremy (Violent J. Caster) in his rookie year in wrestling going up against our current champion "The Human Wrecking ball" Pete Madden. Pete Madden was an excellent wrestler who honestly trained Jeremy and me more than anyone else and he was very smart in the ring and knew how to work the crowd. Jeremy was scheduled to go over that night and win the title belt after a long story of buildup and failure plus the additional benefit of it being in his hometown and rookie year. Two great matches, two entirely different styles with two entirely different payoffs. When it came down to interest level and crowd engagement nothing was going to beat Madman Pondo versus Abdullah the Butcher. Nonetheless, the booking decision was incredibly easy for me so the title match was the main event with Pondo, Abdullah, and me going on before it. A big part of the decision was an idea that I don't know if Jeremy came up with or I did and it truly doesn't matter but with his whole family going to be there at the show, and not told if he was going to win or not, the decision was made to have him request they enter the ring and celebrate with him after his victory. Jeremy had no small family so the visual and more importantly the emotional impact of this was enough to make me definitely move it to the main event. I go over in greater detail the match with Pondo, Abby, and me elsewhere in this book but I will say here that we succeeded 100% in our goal of absolutely blowing away the fans by getting them actively interested in the match and thoroughly engaged. The title match with Jeremy was booked out to achieve the same goal. At intermission when Jeremy was out signing autographs Pete attacked him from behind and repeatedly slammed his ribs into the steel ring post with eventually Jeremy having to take a stretcher ride to the back. Post intermission the Commissioner announced that Jerry's medical condition was unknown at this time and that the crowd would be updated right before this match. After our match, Jeremy was brought out with this entire rib cage bandaged up and "clearly" in pain. He told the commissioners nothing was going to stop him from winning this match and that he didn't care what the doctor said. Obviously, this was all set up to hook the crowd earlier in the evening with the question of whether was Jeremy going to be able to compete or not as many of them may have been compelled to leave after the Pondo/Abby match. An added bonus of the injury angle made it seem even less likely that Jeremy would be winning the match. Pete and Jeremy executed their match perfectly with Pete beating the hell out of Jeremy the entire match constantly cheating and even gloating about how little of a competition this is and that he could pin Jeremy whenever felt like it. Despite all that Jeremy did a reversal late in the match, executed his big move for the pinfall victory and the crowd went absolutely insane and overflowed with emotion as his family came into the ring and hoisted him about their shoulders. Abdullah, Pondo and I were in the back tending to our wounds that we had suffered in our match when we heard the crazy pop when Jeremy won his match and Abdullah asked: "I wonder what that was?" I simply replied "great wrestling (as in a testament to the booking and the wrestlers involved)".

As a follow-up to that story, and in part as a cautionary tale about booking, a few months later I was working in an exploding barbed wire death match for the insane clown posse on one of their strangle mania shows in Detroit that Abdullah the Butcher was also on. I ran in to Abby in the locker room and said "Hey Abby, I don't know if you remember me but I was the manager in your match with Madman Pondo in St. Louis a few months ago". He said he actually did remember me and asked what I was doing there. I said I was there for an exploding barbed wire death match with Madman Pondo and three other guys as it was a tag match. He stated, "oh, that is kind of disappointing". I of course asked why and he said he was hoping I would be involved in the match that he was involved in. I consider this to be the greatest compliment of my entire career and thanked him profusely to which he explained "99% of the time when I do shows they put me with a manager and 99% of those times the manager is the promoter or the promoter's friend or the promoter's kid or just generally someone who has no business in the ring. They embarrass themselves and they make my match that much harder. It was so easy working with you as you clearly knew your role and how to sell it and how to work with the wrestlers as a manager and since that is so rare it would've been great to have that here." You obviously see why that was the greatest compliment of my career but it does also illustrate an important point regarding booking. I mentioned it before but it needs to be stressed you have to take ego out of the equation. Booking decisions must solely be made on what is best for the paying audience not you the booker if you are going to be part of the show.

The third issue to consider when booking the flow of the show that is almost universally ignored is mic work. There is a golden rule to mic work and it is that less is more. I have seen shows where before every single match at least one, and horrifyingly sometimes both, wrestlers must get on the mic and 99% of the time make themselves look ridiculous as they don't know how to do mic work. The issue beyond that of course is it interrupts the flow of the show. You are trying to maintain the willing suspension of disbelief as best you can. Larger-than-life wrestlers should not be talking on the mic for no reason whatsoever or talking in such a fashion that exposes how bad they really are at talking. Again, using a parallel to film and television you must show the audience not tell the audience. Mic work is telling - wrestling is showing. Just like film and television excellent mic work (dialogue) can work wonders to move along the story so my recommendation is not to eliminate it but use it sparingly and wisely. Make sure the individuals doing mic work be it a wrestler or manager have the proper abilities and also ensure that the general outline and content of their speech is going to move the storyline along. I am 100% against scripts so I'm not recommending telling people exactly what to say as they need to be able to say things as their character would but there should be a general outline and more importantly a goal that this mic work is supposed to follow and/or accomplish.

23

THE CROWD

(what they want and stop ignoring them)

24

I want to make this very simple and very clear right off the bat you must always keep in mind the crowd wants to be entertained. It is that simple and at the same time that incredibly complex. The first thing to keep in mind is that, like a movie or concert or any other form of entertainment, the paying audience is doing so in order to be distracted from the doldrums of their normal life. They want to see things they don't normally see in their everyday life. Feel things they don't normally feel. Be affected in ways they are not expecting to be affected. The next question that most people ask is "okay, so how do I get them that?" For starters, I recommend following everything that's come in this book before this section. Reread it if you must with an eye for observing the psychological concepts that are discussed and covered. It is all been geared toward eliciting a response from the crowd. This at its core is what they want. They want to be sucked in by the story. They want to believe. They want to experience vicariously the highs and lows of the heroes while despising and wishing ill will upon the villains. I can't give you a formula or plan or framework that will help you accomplish this because the beauty of professional wrestling is that no such limitations exist. You're free to create any story - you just have to make sure that it is relatable and entertaining and that it follows a logical progression having a beginning, a middle, and an end. This formula has worked from the moment man conveyed morality tales orally to each other, through written texts, and up to all of today's modern entertainment options.

A word of caution regarding what might define as "the crowd". What I have seen time and time again are wrestlers and bookers who consciously or subconsciously have decided that the crowd is them. That is to say, they think that the crowd wants to see what they would like to see. The great danger in this is of course the fact that the view from inside the business is radically different than the view from outside it. A wrestler may become extremely proficient in their craft and so to them an insanely complex 20-move Japanese finish may be the pinnacle of what they desire to see but 99% of the paying audience have no concept or appreciation of such a complex finish and would not only care less but in fact be turned off by their failure to follow such a complex string of events. The other death blow that I have seen struck against more than one promotion is when the promoter decides to instill their personal values in the stories. Making no judgment on whether the position is right or wrong if you hold social or political values that are at or near the extreme then infusing them in your storylines alienates a large section of your crowd. If you're ultraconservative or extremely liberal you make sure that your stories don't reflect that or risk turning off not just the people that don't agree with you but a large segment of the people who do for the simple fact that they are going to an entertainment venue for the expressed reason of not having to think about or deal with those political/social ideologies. You must always remember the crowd is just here to have fun. They are not there to think, be ridiculed, informed, insulted, or be confused. THEY ARE JUST THERE TO HAVE FUN!

The crowd is also not just one "type" of person. Not everyone in the crowd hates their significant other. Not everyone in the crowd hates their job. People like to make the argument that perhaps "most" people in the crowd feel this way or that way but you honestly have no way of knowing that. The smart move, and one of the primary advantages of having multiple matches on a wrestling card, is that you're able to book stories that appeal to different types of people. Having an angle with a love triangle in one match and an angle with a disrespected friend in another ensures your ability to appeal to a wide range of people for a quick and basic example. The key is to, for lack of a better word, "key" into core concepts that all humans share. Jealousy, anger, honor, and justice are just a few of the key components that make us who we are. Yes, we all have different definitions of those ideas and levels of intensity but we all share them at a core level. If a face wrestler is out to get justice for a perceived wrong by the heel different members of the audience may not agree on whether the wrong truly deserves justice or not however both will be able to understand the face's desire to acquire that justice. You must first think in broad strokes when determining what the audience wants to see and once you have that laid out then you can start to book specifics and the minutia that supports and ties in everything to create the overarching concept. Here is a quick breakdown - everyone likes to reference the attitude era of the WWE with the Vince McMahon and Stone Cold Steve Austin feud. Even though it went on for years, contained a myriad of twists and turns, and from time to time involved other wrestlers, the overarching concept at its core was the common man getting one over on his asshole boss. Everything they did in that angle was at the service of that concept and that is a perfect core concept for the bulk of the audience to relate to. There may be someone in the audience that loves their boss but it doesn't mean that every boss they've ever had they have loved or if by some miracle they have it doesn't mean they've never known a close relative or friend who did have a boss they hated and constantly bitched about. Any way you slice it everyone has an ability to relate to and/or understand that overarching concept. That angle gave the audience exactly what they wanted - the ability to be distracted, engaged, and drawn in to a stimulating storyline and to see good defeat evil while easily imprinting on the good (Austin) and again, by far the most important – have fun doing it.

Another very important aspect of the crowd that gets overlooked a lot is that they want to be surprised. Having a big twist in an angle or introducing some out-of-this-world character can be a nice little surprise and they are effective but I'm referring to a more global concept of surprising. One of the things that I would do whenever showing up to a venue is survey the venue layout, the placement of the ring, the layout of chairs, the strength and composition of the guardrails, and anything else that I could find that might open up something new and different that the crowd has not seen before. When going over matches with wrestlers there was also a concerted effort to try to come up with not just one but a few things in the match that the crowd had never seen before and I'm not talking about some big twisty off-the-top rope move either. I'll give an example of both types so you have a better understanding. Previously I mentioned the match where there were some abandoned lockers in a National Guard Armory that were utilized in the finish. This match was to be a falls count anywhere, no disqualification blow-off match for a feud so the first thing I said when the two wrestlers involved sat down to go over the match was we needed to come up with a way to eliminate me from the match early on. This was a blowout so the match needed to be solely focused on them without the distraction of the heel manager. This was primarily done since I had spent the entirety of the feud being involved and causing issues. This also was a setup for the next feud as it gave me the opportunity to say if I had been involved in the match things would have gone differently. Regardless the discussion was made and I put forth the following idea: we start the match immediately by dumping to the outside of the ring, spilling over the guardrail fighting in the crowd, and making our way over towards the lockers which had been positioned standing up against a wall of the Armory – just like in school. Once there the face would execute a big move on the heel thus temporarily taking him out of the picture and I would jump on the back of the face who would then grab my legs so that he was effectively carrying me and walk backward into the concrete wall crushing me. He would then walk over, open one of the lockers, point to the inside then point to me seeking the crowd's approval after which he would pick me up and whip me into the locker. The locker was large enough to fit me so he would then proceed to close the door. That all sounds good and funny as it plays to the jock locking the nerd in his locker in high school but I suggested that such an act was not the final step. The final step is that once I was in the locker and the door was closed, he would push the locker over with me inside it. That was a devastating enough move to ensure that I would be out of the picture until the finish of the match and not something the crowd had seen before. This is the point where some people state that I have just been hypocritical as I previously admonished wrestlers for plotting out every single move and hold that they were going to do and I have effectively just done that. My defense is that this sequence was not setting up a wrestling match but was utilizing specific tools to accomplish the goal of removing me as an influence on their match. Keep reading and you'll see how things did not go according to plan. Back to the day of the show, following the three rules and needing to protect myself I examined the interior of the lockers prior to suggesting this and found three hooks, one in the back and one on each side that was obviously used to hang clothes in the locker but could do a tremendous amount of damage to me either when I was whipped into the locker or when it came crashing down as they were pretty much at head height so a screwdriver was procured and the hooks removed. During the match, there was an important addition that I feel needs to be pointed out to give you an idea of the way things should be. I knew both wrestlers incredibly well and they were both extreme professionals and at the top of their game so while they did their parts perfectly, things did not go exactly according to plan. After the face backed me into the concrete wall someone in the crowd handed the face a hard plastic shovel I think used for gardening. It was full-size - not like the little tiny shovel you would use at the beach. Without saying a word, the face picked me up and gave me a punch. Now I knew and understood that he was going to need a little bit of time to grab the shovel by both hands and play to the crowd as I imagine his plan was to hit me with it. I also am aware there is nothing worse than watching a wrestler stand there waiting to get hit. Without saying a word and operating on the idea that this very high-quality wrestler knew exactly what I was doing I staggered and spun around in a 360° arc at such a speed and distance so that by the time I was facing him again I would be expecting to get hit by a plastic shovel and that is exactly what happened as he was able to pick up on what I was doing and adjust the speed and timing of the shovel swing to match my spinning. None of this was planned and none of it was even called between us, it was simply a matter of two wrestlers (okay I'll be honest a wrestler and a manager) operating at a level where they knew what was going to work best without having to have a plan or discussion about it. The feeling of working with wrestlers at that level is indescribable but the goal if you follow everything in this book.

The second surprise item that you should you familiarize yourself with are sequences that you have that you know work and you can use any time you are in front of a new crowd. These are things that usually only work one time and are often comedy related but when done properly comedy bits can be some of the most effective in all of wrestling. Put all your sensitivity and political correctness aside as I introduce you to the butt fuck spot (even if offended, read on to the end – pun intended). This is one of several sequences that we had in our back pocket (again, pun intended) and utilized every single time we went into a new town. It is simple and never failed to elicit a great response. This does require male wrestlers and a manager and it is usually done somewhat early on in the match when the heel manager interferes but is cut off by the face and whipped into the corner with their back to the corner. The manager doesn't really sell it too much but merely positions themselves in the corner standing sort of propped up by the top ring ropes under their armpits. Either through a reversal or just a usual whip (dealers' choice), the heel wrestler is then whipped into the heel manager in the corner slamming the heel wrestler's back into the heel manager's chest. The heel wrestler will then fall forward so that they are on all fours. After a second or two the heel manager who had been shaking and selling the impact of being crushed by the heel wrestler will fall on his knees behind the heel wrestler positioning his crotch against the heel's rear end and continuing to shake such that it looks like to the audience that he is having anal sex with his heel wrestler. After a few gyrations, the heel wrestler will jump up, ask or mime a "what the hell" then shove the heel manager o would then roll outside the ring and the face is usually best poised to do a quick inside cradle roll up for a two count. Back in the day, this was a great comedy spot because homosexuality was looked down upon and it was the heel engaging in such activity. Today it is a great comedy spot in some areas of the country where homosexuality is still looked down upon and in areas where it is not actually considered rude or insulting to be offended by such activity it does make the heels look bad as well due to their bigotry and closed-mindedness. Regardless of your position (pun intended yet again) on homosexuality the spot works either way. This is but a single example and we had about a dozen including different ones for tag teams or single wrestlers and ones for rural crowds and others for more cosmopolitan audiences but we always had them to be used in front of the new crowd.

The second subtitle to this section is to stop ignoring the crowd. This deserves particular focus as this is the #1 offense that I find 95% of wrestlers today are guilty of. As you have seen me illustrate in this book, I regularly see matches where wrestlers have no other look on their face or body language than one that says "I'm just waiting for my turn to do wrestling moves". To every one of these wrestlers, I simply say - get over yourself. If your concern is how well you can do a wrestling hold or how much you can impress other wrestlers with your wrestling skill then please tell me why you are not working for free in the training center with other wrestlers that think as you do? With that mindset, there is no reason for you to get paid and no reason for you to subject an audience to your ego stroke. Having asked some of these wrestlers that very question the answer that I invariably received is because they want to get feedback from the audience. That is a bald-faced lie and at best it is them lying to themselves. I also need to make this very clear to avoid the inevitable copout that a lot of these wrestlers put forth and that is my definition of "ignoring the crowd". First and foremost, it is not absolute. These types of wrestlers will try to stand on the technical definition and say I don't ignore the crowd because I insulted them when I came down to the ring or slapped their wrists as a face when I came to the ring, etc. If that was all you had to do to "engage the crowd" then sure, you did not ignore the crowd. Obviously from the lack of interest displayed by the crowd for those wrestlers' matches, it is not all you have to do. The best mindset to have is that you need to engage the crowd constantly. I'm not saying after every move or hold but you need to make a point to acknowledge them on a regular basis. While this is primarily the job of the heel, and by far the easiest for them, the face is not exempt from engaging the crowd. To give you an idea of just how bad this is there is one simple move that is a no-brainer that should be done every single time. This move is so simple and important that there is no way that today's wrestlers did not grow up without seeing it or have not watched grade A wrestling matches without seeing it. This is going to sound ridiculous but after a face wins a match - especially a title match or the feud blowout match - they must immediately go to the ropes or turnbuckle and engage the crowd. By engaging the crowd I don't mean a simple quick look or raise of the belt, I mean a prolonged and deep desire to connect with them and make them a part of the victory. The knee-jerk reaction from most wrestlers I've seen is that the statement is ridiculous and they see that all the time even in crappy indy promotions but I encourage you to go to the next show with a slightly different eye and check to see how many face wrestlers after their victory genuinely engage (remember, not merely pay lip service) to the crowd. Even if half of them do and half of them don't that still is a terrible percentage. Remember, as a wrestler, you are there for the audience and they are there to vicariously live through you so if the face wrestler has a victory they need to make sure that the audience gets to share in that moment. Engaging the crowd can take place in a variety of ways and one of the best that I point out to other wrestlers, and have referenced previously in this book, is when the face will start to no sell light moves like punches eventually completely no selling and then taking over on the heel. Many wrestlers such as Hulk Hogan and Jerry "The King" Lawler used this to build an entire career. Most of these modern wrestlers scoff at such actions as being silly or "old-school". The problem is of course that they are neither and that they continue to work regardless of what year it is when reading this book - it will always work. Everyone in the crowd would like to think that when they're getting beat down, they will somehow muster up the intestinal fortitude and strength to stand up and not take it anymore. The face starting to no sell a little bit builds anticipation in the audience members that perhaps they are about to see that very idea and when eventually they do and the face completely no sells the offense the audience immediately keys in to that core concept and are completely engaged. As the face had just been beaten down it doesn't make sense if it's an instant come back so the slow build-up becomes part of the sell. Some wrestlers I've told this to have tried it and it "failed" so I sadly have to add for this to work you have to be over in the first place! The crowd has to care about you for anything to work! The other place where it is not only incredibly easy but an absolute must to engage the crowd is during rest holds. Yet again I must point out that I rarely see this being utilized. I don't care if it's the chin lock or figure 4 leg lock or Boston crab the wrestler who is not selling the move needs to be acknowledging the crowd in alignment with their face/heel persona. There is no excuse to not take advantage of this custom-built scenario where you don't have to worry about anything other than engaging the crowd. You and your opponent are both resting and the move is structured such that one of you have the undivided attention of the crowd. I also wanted to address the idea of "accidental engagement" as I'm seeing more and more of this and sadly, I'm also seeing more and more wrestlers commenting on this by claiming credit for it. If you as a wrestler are engaged in something and the crowd suddenly starts to react to it without intent from you, then you have not actually engaged the crowd. A very simple explanation of this that I've seen many, many times is that a wrestler will have another in the ropes punch them repeatedly such that after the third or fourth punch the crowd starts to count. 5, 6, 7 all building up to a big punch on 10. The wrestler did not engage the audience, the audience engaged the wrestler based on previous behavior they have seen or been part of – ie: we always count when someone is punching people in the corner repeatedly. Flipping that around in the other direction is the easiest thing in the world. If a face heads over to a heel standing prone in the corner and grabs them by the hair in one hand, they can use the other hand to ball a fist, raise into the air, and ask the audience if they want them to give this to the heel. Don't accept the first "yes" instead ask a second time which if done properly should elicit a more enthusiastic response that can then be followed up with the audience counting along the punches but this time starting from the first one and building up to the last. The audience is drawn in from the onset by the wrestler and enthusiastically moves along with the structure of the beating. Such a scenario is going to garner a far better response than one where the audience felt they had to force themselves, or it was merely a habit, to be a part of the activity.

I mentioned before that a large number of wrestlers will comment upon the fact that they think my suggestions are silly or "old-school". I've even quite often heard the phrase "that doesn't work with modern audiences". What I have been pointing out and will continue to point out in this book are core psychological concepts and ideas that work on human beings. They work on human beings now, they worked on human beings 30 years ago, 100 years ago even a thousand years ago and they will continue to work on humans for the foreseeable future. It took hundreds of thousands of years of evolution to establish the core concepts of humanity so I suspect it will take another few hundreds of thousands of years to change them. To clear things up, what many of the wrestlers who dismiss the ideas will probably boast of is that wrestling has changed over the years and as such, the audience has changed as well. For example in the 1920s, 1930s, and even 1940s, wrestling matches almost looked like amateur bouts and could go on for hours and rarely if ever involved any move off the top rope. They will claim that if you were to do a similar match today the audience would be bored and tune out. It is a fact that technical aspects of such a match - mostly amateur wrestling moves, rest holds, and groundwork - would be boring today but the wrestlers stating that fail to see what else was going on in those matches. I had a few occasions where I got to illustrate this perfectly. I invited one of these wrestlers with that viewpoint to watch with me a classic match from that time period - or more accurately five minutes of the match as that's usually all they can take - and then once they get done complaining about how dull and boring it is, I asked them who was the face and who was the heel? They are always able to quickly and accurately tell me which is which. I then asked why and regardless of the answer we watch the match again through the lens of what actions the wrestlers are taking that are not wrestling-related to establish to the crowd and to us the viewer they are a face or heel. Each and every time the actions they engage in are the exact same actions that great wrestlers 50 years later and even today can utilize to get themselves over with the crowd. They cheat, they engage, they have false comebacks, personas they key into core concepts, etc. All these things I mention in this book have been going on in wrestling for over a hundred years but more importantly, the psychological concepts of what entertains humans have been the same for thousands of years, and to ignore that or think things have changed will result in little to no reaction from a crowd.

HOW TO BLEED

(and when and why)

26

There used to be a great saying in the territory days of professional wrestling which was "red means green". A translation for those that have never heard the phrase is that if the audience saw red (blood) they were much more likely to cough up green(money). Primarily used at that point in time for blowoff matches or to establish serious injury a lot of the impact was lost during the 90s with the hard-core years and also throughout the 80s and 90s and 00s due to health scares related to HIV, Hepatitis, and more. It now seems to have almost completely gone away due to either the ignorance of how to do it or the fear of doing it however the fact that it has a real impact on the audience has not changed.

The real reason why bleeding was so successful and continues to be to this day - if used properly - is because it establishes reality greater than any other activity. Although it is almost completely out of the realm of my experience (with one exception that I will note later) I am not referring to fake blood. Fake blood really only works in a single instance that I will mention but otherwise, for all other intents and purposes, in order to establish reality, the blood must be real. Everyone in that audience has been cut and bled so they know exactly what it looks like. They know how blood flows, know how it coagulates, they know its color, its consistency, and when they see that on a wrestler, regardless of their view on kayfabe, they know it's real. That realism does more to support and reinforce the willing suspension of disbelief than almost anything else. It doesn't matter if they think that the wrestler cut themselves, they still can't argue or convince themselves that the blood is not real or that there is not someone in that ring (or outside of it) that is legitimately bleeding for one reason or another. As an added bonus, if it is the face that is bleeding (and honestly it almost always should be) the audience as a bonus knows what it's like to feel the pain of being cut and bleeding so they are able to further empathize and vicariously live through the face. Blood should also be used sparingly in order to increase the impact. Just as I mentioned before that I would blacklist certain moves from occurring for an entire show because they were going to be important in a match at the end of the show bleeding should also be regulated and not occur every match. I would even go several cards without any blood at all for it to then be used on a blow-off match on one card. The fact that the audience had not seen it not only in previous matches but entire shows granted greater impact due to its rarity and a certain element of surprise as it isn't something the audience was not used to or expecting to see. Utilizing it in a big blow off the match further immerses the crowd as, if the feud has been done properly, the crowd should actually want to see the heel's blood (at the very least) giving you an opportunity to provide them that cathartic experience again the heel or you can manipulate them further by blood being done to the face instead when they least expected it and/or wanted it.

I mentioned the one exception for the use of fake blood and that is when trying to really sell an internal injury which is not often the easiest of things. Internal injuries need to be set up well in advance either through a series of matches or as the main focus of a single match. The basic idea is that some part of the body that is not a limb has been worked on to the point where one final devastating move causes the individual to spit blood. This obviously doesn't leave a lot of options so it is pretty much the chest or the back. To illustrate this, one time in a singles match we had the basic setup of very early into the match the heel on the outside of the ring whipped the face into one of the steel support beams chest first which the face sold tremendously. During the rest of the match when the heel was up he made sure to be attacking the chest or administering clotheslines to the chest. A big devastating move by the heel with a little cheating resulted in the face being pinned and also unable to recover. At the time, we had solid steel ring steps that consisted of two parts. The bottom part had a step and then two legs on each side of the step with an opening where the second part went over that opening to provide the second step. The steps were quite wide in fact probably wider than they should have been but that actually worked to our advantage in this case. While celebrating our victory in the ring I as the manager rolled to the outside of the ring, split the ring stairs into two parts, and then proceeded to lift onto the apron and pushed into the ring the bottom section. As a side note, the workers involved were of such a level that the final move and pinfall resulted in the face being dead center facing the stationary camera. The heel took the bottom of the stair steps that I had put into the ring so that the legs of the open area were on either side of the chest of the face on the ground with each leg sort of being just below the armpits if you can picture it. He then proceeded to lift the step and slam it back into the chest of the face. Prior to the match, we tested the length of the legs to ensure that it would appear to a certain extent the chest would be hit by the steps since if the legs were too long it would appear that the chest was not hit to the audience. At this point you might be saying isn't this supposed to be about fake blood? Well at the moment that the heel brought the lower stair portion down across the face's chest the face sprayed blood straight up in the air from a blood capsule I had slipped him while appearing to be insulting him to his face after the pin. The reason this worked was primarily due to the fact that he was far enough away from the crowd to avoid close inspection and for the fact that very few if any people in the audience ever had internal bleeding and spit up blood in such a fashion so they would not know whether that was realistic or not. Being aligned with the hard camera ensured that a great video shot of it was taken since a close-up shot could easily reveal what was going on with the fake blood. To further sell the angle and protect the illusion, several other faces came out after this to run off me and the heel wrestler, and they then each took a shoulder of the face to prop up and walked out the back. The reason they did this was to obscure the view of the audience so that they would see blood coming down the front of his mouth and covering his shirt but never get a clear look and never really even be able to see the color, texture, consistency, etc.

So that pretty much covers the when and why so now will get into the how. You will invariably run across wrestlers who have their favorite method of blading (wrestler slang for cutting oneself) and I will give you mine and the reason why I prefer it but it will be very important to first cover the don'ts when it comes to blading as so many wrestlers make these mistakes. First and foremost, do not take an aspirin before blading. To this day I see what are perceived to be veteran wrestlers telling rookie wrestlers to do this because they will bleed more. While they are technically correct if the wrestler has any kind of issue with blood coagulating this could cause serious harm but beyond that, the flow of the blood tends to be too much which impacts its credibility and possibly the wrestler's ability to see since too much blood in running into their eyes. As previously stated, we have to remember most people in the audience have cut themselves accidentally at some point so they know exactly what it looks like and how it flows so seeing a gusher is going to blow the illusion that this happened due to an injury and not on purpose. The next word of advice from these so-called veterans that often see is instructions to do it when your head is covered so that people don't see you doing the cutting. They recommend going under the ring or being under the announced table or crouching down between the stair steps in the ring apron. This falls under the category of a bad special effect using our movie analogy. At the movies, even though the audience is engaging in willing suspension of disbelief as soon as they see some poorly done special effect it ruins that illusion and the same holds true when you obviously are hiding your face in order to cut yourself. Wrestlers will also have a variety of different places where you should hide your blade and sadly, I have heard this on more than one occasion so a big don't is this - don't hide your blade in your mouth. I know that sounds insane but I have heard that advice given out on more than one occasion. So how do I prepare, store, apply, and hide my blade?

Preparing a blade is actually extremely important and something I have also seen go horribly wrong. There will be pictures to illustrate this to follow. The best scenario I have found is to take a double-edge straight razor blade and using scissors cut at an angle an approximately 1 inch to 1 ½ inches long slice. You then want to take a roll of athletic tape and, leaving approximately one-eighth to at most one-quarter of an inch of the sharp edge exposed and wrap a thin sliver of athletic tape around it about three times. This is arguably one of the most important steps as what I have seen countless times is an exposed sharp edge that is half-inch an inch or even more. If you do that invariably you're going to cut far, far too deep which can easily lead to greater scarring. Continuing with the preparation I will take that wrapped sliver and lay it down on my dominant index finger with the exposed blade portion protruding the full 1/8 to 1/4 inch beyond the tip. Again, using athletic tape, I will then wrap around that finger anchoring it in place. I then take a small portion of athletic tape folded into a small square approximately ¼ to ½ inch and about three folds deep. Place that square in the middle of a 3-inch strip of athletic tape and fold that tape over your finger such that the square goes over the exposed blade. Keeping one side of the tape attached to the tape on the finger and the other free to wrap around the finger twice further securing the top portion of that 3-inch strip that you have attached. As for the dangling part fold, ¼ inch of the tip over on itself and then the adhesive will go down the other side. What you have now is a situation whereby the blade is covered and protected such that you can go about the whole match doing any moves, holds, counter moves and counter holds that you need to without any concern of any accidental cutting of yourself or your opponent and with it looking like your fingers are taped up as usual - operating on the idea that you usually go to the ring with tape on your fingers (which I can't recommend enough that you do since not only will it make this blade selling perfect but also give you better grip in the match which is quite useful all around). When the time comes for you to blade, simply pull the folded-over quarter-inch strip exposing the sharp blade, cut yourself, then fold the tape back over and no one is the wiser. The other advantage of this method that honestly can't be replicated in other methods is the fact that you only have a 1/8 to 1/4 inch length of blade exposed and therefore that is the total depth that can be penetrated into your skin unless you push way too hard and at the wrong angle. The short blade is all that is needed to cause you to bleed and it helps in reducing the scarring. Speaking of reducing the scarring the next thing I'll cover is one of the most important - where to cut yourself. Most wrestlers will tell you to cut your forehead. If they've been in the business for a while and are even a little bit savvy, they may additionally tell you to run the blade left to right such that it can blend in with the future wrinkles in your forehead. These wrestlers are not exactly wrong but there is a much better way to do it. The best way is to cut yourself above your hairline. Direction is pretty much irrelevant at that point though left to the right reduces the chance you will cut below the hairline. The blood will still run down your face giving the illusion that you are cut in the forehead however any issues concerning scarring will ideally be covered by your hair later in life. Yes, this assumes that you won't have a receding hairline or go bald but either way this at least gives you a fighting chance to not wind up with a scarred-up forehead should you be in the business long enough and do enough blading. This goes out the window of course if you are bald or cutting a different body part. A quick note about cutting other body parts. Though you can certainly do it, I would argue it is fundamentally pointless. There is a certain visceral reaction from the crowd seeing blood run down the face of a wrestler. First of all, the face of the wrestlers tends to be a focal point for the attention of the audience. Yes, they are watching moves and holds, but at the end of the day, the expression on the face be it anger, sadness, joy, pain, etc. is what really creates and maintains the emotional connection as well as conveys important aspects of the story. Blood running down a face amplifies those expressions as the stakes are much higher now that an injury has occurred. Having a cut on your arm or leg can barely be seen and as that arm or leg is involved in moves and holds unless the cut is deep (which you don't want) the blood will also not be able to be seen at all after a while. I know just reading the text on how to create a blade may be difficult if you have to visualize it yourself in my explanations may not be 100% clear so here is a visual representation of how to create the blade that I used for years without fail:

Needed Items

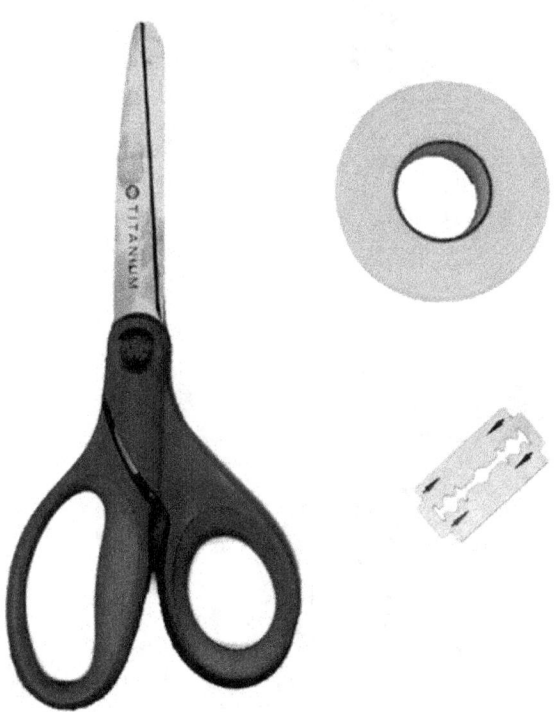

Cut the straight Razor

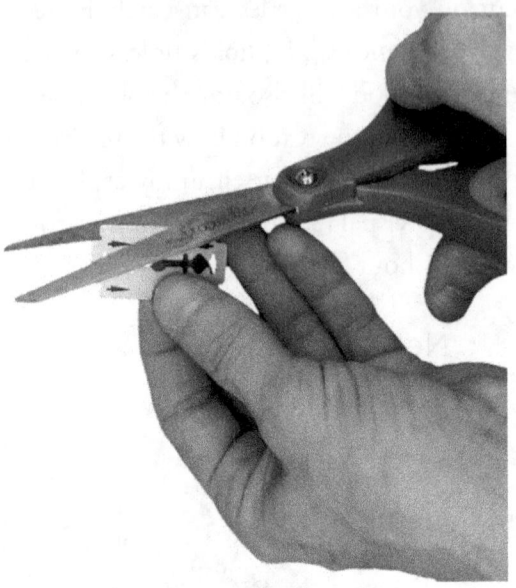

Size of the cut blade

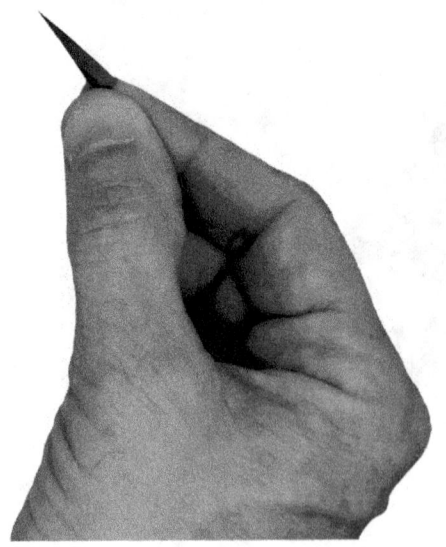

Wrap the blade

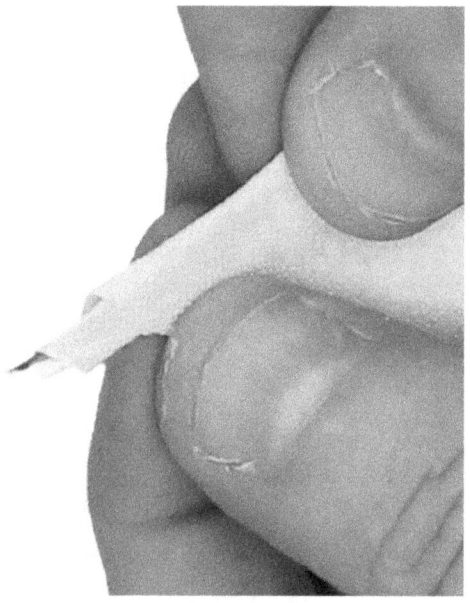

Attach blade to tip of finger

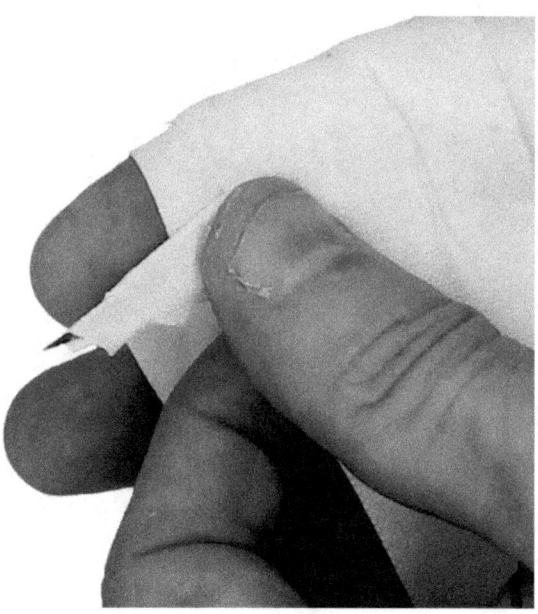

Measure out a single strip

Blade placement on the wrap

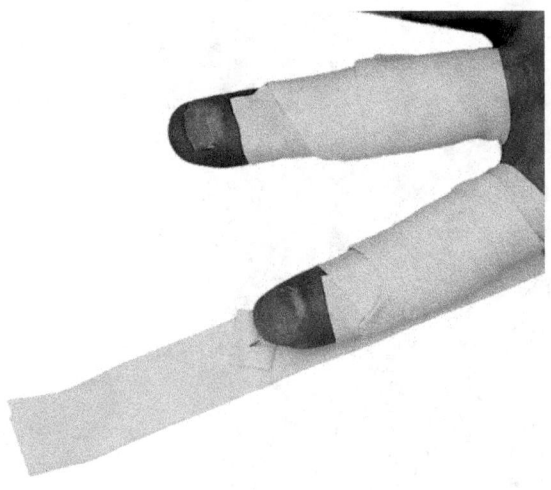

Safety wrapped and ready for match

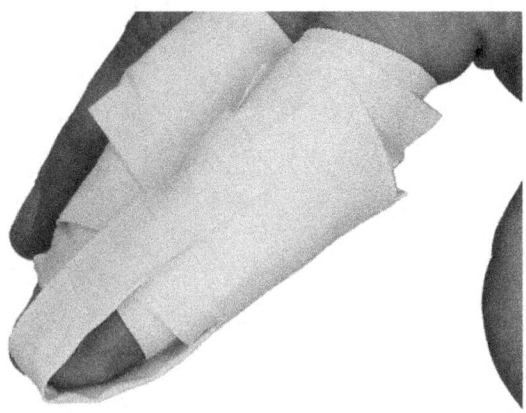

MATCH TYPES

(build up and conclusion)

28

There are of course an infinite number of match types in professional wrestling however the how and why of some of the most common ones seems to have been overlooked, altered, or just plain wrong to modern-day wrestlers and more importantly audiences. Outlined here are a handful of them and I'll explain their purpose and some booking ideas to consider.

BATTLE ROYAL

The Battle Royal and its distant cousin the Royal Rumble is the highest utility match of all the gimmick matches. You have a very wide range of options as to how to further a storyline or multiple storylines via a single match. On the surface, you have a number of wrestlers in the ring with mixed allegiances and of course, the heels always double-cross everyone, solely out for themselves. Ultimately the only thing that really matters in a Battle Royal is the last 2 to 4 people. The best three scenarios are that the parties involved should have either recently ended a feud, currently, be in a feud or you have plans to spin off a new feud with them. Bonus booking for any combination of those three. The options are infinite but the important booking factors are who gets eliminated when and why. Remember it is always about the "why". What prize is on the line for the winner of the Battle Royal also plays a factor in how it will be booked out. What I often see is that a title is awarded to the winner of the match. Many bookers think this raises the stakes but without a good reason as to why it doesn't. First, you need to establish some reason that the title belt is in dispute and/or a reason as to why the current title holder would consent to such a match or why the current title holder is being forced to participate in the match. Bonus points if you have a face champion forced to put up his belt in the Battle Royal and you run an injury angle preventing them from taking place in the match ensuring that there will be a new champion and high motivation to regain their belt since not only in the face's mind but the crowds as well, they never lost the belt themselves. You could have two faces as the last two people in the ring, you could have a face and a heel currently engaged in their own feud as the last two people thus either spinning off the new feud or starting to incorporate one or both into existing feuds, etc., etc. - as you can see the options are limitless. The main issue with booking a Battle Royal, and the reason the Royal Rumble came into existence, is that you must book out the order and method of elimination for all wrestlers involved. If everyone is in the ring at the same time you run the risk of the audience not seeing an elimination or having eliminations too close together eliminating the effect of elimination (so to speak). The Royal Rumble's method of staggering the entrance time of participants is the workaround for this.

NO DISQUALIFICATION

Many wrestlers have told me that there is no point in a no disqualification match since very few if any rules which would result in disqualification are ever enforced. This is one of the rare instances where they might be right. It then falls to the booker to craft a storyline where not having disqualification means something. On a very simple level you could have the heel when they are clearly outmatched and about to lose, deliberately be caught cheating in order to be disqualified two or a maximum of three times before setting up the no disqualification match. You will however have to have a good reason for the heel to accept such a match as they have been relying on it to not have an embarrassing loss to the face. Another simple one is to have a list of moves that are banned in the promotion for example the piledriver. Having matches where the heel teases piledriving the face but is always stopped by a referee or other party would motivate them to accept a no disqualification match because then they will be able to do the piledriver without losing the match. Bonus points for booking the match such that the heel has three failed attempts at a piledriver and the face executes the move flawlessly once for the victory.

STEEL CAGE

The Steel Cage match is one of the most misunderstood matches out there. In modern times the idea seems to be that the Steel Cage is there to keep the wrestlers inside. In reality, the origin of the Steel Cage match was that it was designed to keep other wrestlers out. Through storyline buildup, there had been so much interference and so many cross storylines -which there should be - that it was determined the only way to settle things was to lock two or more wrestlers inside the cage and let them battle it out until there was a clear winner. There was no stipulation about having to climb out of the cage and have your feet touch the floor or anything like that as the cage was used as a tool to ensure a definitive outcome - at least in the audience's eyes that is. With the proper booking, it can return to that glorious function. Simply laying down the rules to the audience in such a way that this is what they want to see creates much higher drama and interest from the audience than all this silliness about climbing out of the cage. The main issue with having to climb out of the cage and have your feet touch the floor is that despite hundreds of matches, rarely if ever has there been one that when one wrestler was trying to get over the top of the cage while the other was laying prone in the middle of the ring, or if they were both together at the top of the cage - it didn't look absolutely ridiculous and made no sense as to why one or the other wrestler didn't take a quick way out as far as the audience is concerned. Having to slowly climb up the cage, perch at the top, and then slowly climb your way back down so that the opponent selling in the ring has time to recover and cut you off completely destroys the willing suspension of disbelief as it makes 100% sense to simply fall – not climb down - from the top of the cage as you will quickly find your feet on the floor and be declared the winner. Simultaneously fighting while climbing up the cage or at the top of the cage also completely destroys the willing suspension of disbelief as the participants must be so careful while doing these things so that they don't fall and mess up that it comes off as being very unconvincing and it is clear that they are in fact being careful trying not to fall. It might look absolutely spectacular but everyone in the audience is asking themselves why, when the wrestler climbs to the top of the cage and then turns around and executes some big move onto their opponent inside the ring, they didn't just drop to the floor to win. Flip the script and if you only win a cage match by pinning your opponent it actually makes 100% sense for a wrestler to jump off the top of the cage onto their opponent in the ring as that would inflict maximum damage. Need any further proof? One of the most successful variations on the Steel Cage match is War Games. For those unfamiliar, this was a match that took place over two rings both encased in a single Steel Cage however the Steel Cage had a roof. Generally, it would be 8 to 10 people fighting in these rings but of course, the important point is that being completely enclosed they were unable to get out. The victory was achieved via pinfall as it should be and these are generally considered some of the best cage matches of all time – well, the early ones anyway.

TEXAS DEATH MATCH

Having fallen out of favor in recent times the Texas death match provided a large array of different options and concepts that could be executed in the match. Since it has rarely been seen recently, I'll explain the basic premise. Two feuding wrestlers have a long (usually around 12 feet) strap of leather secured around each other's wrist thus connecting the two. Victory is achieved only when one of the wrestlers is able to touch all four ring corners in succession. Hopefully can see a myriad of possibilities opening up. The leather strap can obviously be used as a weapon - you can beat your opponent with it, use it for leverage, wrap it around their neck and choke them, etc., etc. The heel could remove the leather strap from their wrist and secure it around a ring rope or turnbuckle thus limiting the movement of the face. The list goes on and on with only the booker's/wrestler's imagination as a limitation and of course, the most classic ending of them all finds the face in bad shape and the heel having to drag the face behind them as they go and touch the turnbuckle to turnbuckle - imagine them back-to-back with the heel holding the face against his back via the leather strap with one hand and then touching the turnbuckles with the other. As the heel is making their way to each corner and tapping it the face is also tapping the corner behind the heel's back - both literally and figuratively. Just before the heel is able to tap the fourth turnbuckle and win, the face has recovered enough to pull off a reversal, and after some teasing the face touches the turnbuckle winning the match with the heel going absolutely crazy because as far as they are concerned the face has only touched one turnbuckle - remember they were not able to see the other three touches - and lost the match on top of it.

FIRST BLOOD MATCH

Another rarely seen match these days the first blood match is a great way to have a big match in the middle of the feud and still maintain momentum to a larger payout. First and foremost, when announcing the first blood match to your audience you have guaranteed - in the eyes of the audience at least, but easily booked around (though I would recommend against it) – that at least one wrestler will bleed and they will see blood. This is the bare minimum expectation that the audience has and why I recommend against booking some nonsense that deprives them of seeing blood. You're not guaranteeing them a winner or loser just that someone will bleed and not delivering on such a low bar does damage to the expectation that you'll be delivering on the big picture. The classic ending to the match is a slight ref bump that puts them down just long enough for the heel to bloody up the face but with a quick comeback, the face is able to smear their blood on the head of the heel such that when the referee recovers, they only see the blood on the heel and they call the match. Many other finishes are available but there must be blood involved somehow.

BELT SUSPENDED FROM THE RING

This is another match similar to the Steel Cage match where the rules have changed over time. Currently, the focus seems to be entirely on setting up a ladder so that you can climb up it and grab a belt that is suspended very high above the ring. This creates a very similar problem as the Steel Cage Match in that you always have spots where someone is climbing up the ladder in a disproportionately slow manner just so the other opponent can recover and cut them off thus destroying the willing suspension of disbelief with the crowd or you have wrestlers doing some extremely complicated move on the ladder forcing them to be cautious and again destroying willing suspension of disbelief. The way the belt suspended from the ring match is supposed to work is to have a pole in one of the ring corners with a hook the belt can be hung from that is at a height such that any wrestler standing on the top turnbuckle could grab it. Storyline wise you would have to come up or some angle that resulted in a legitimate claim on both sides as to ownership of the belt. The belt that will be held up is then suspended from the hook and the first person in the match to grab it becomes the champion. This creates some very fun and interesting scenarios to play with. First and foremost, pinfalls and disqualifications become completely meaningless thus it allows for the wrestlers to primarily focus on beating the holy hell out of each other or inflicting some big injury that would prevent the opponent from being able to get up and take the belt. Since victory is not achieved via pinfall you automatically have the built-in storyline of either the heel bringing this up angrily or the face bringing it up matter-of-factly to further the feud as the belt did not change hands on a pinfall.

FACE GETS 5 MINUTES WITH THE HEEL MANAGER

Since the heel manager should be constantly interfering in matches and helping the heel wrestler cheat to win you can creatively book a story where if the face wins the match, they get five minutes alone in the ring with the heel manager in order to exact their revenge and some similarly high stake is agreed to by the face if they lose. The ending for such a match is almost always the same in that the face wins the match and yet through interference or some technicality does not get any time with the heel manager or at best one move. This imparts a great frustration on the audience as they were looking forward to seeing the heel manager get their ass kicked. There is of course the practical explanation for this as almost all heel managers are not trained professional wrestlers and as such, it would look absolutely silly for them to hang for five minutes in the ring. This does raise a bit of an issue however as wrestling audiences have been burnt so many times that they now expect for some swerve to happen to deny them seeing the heel manager being beaten up that it has lost almost all effectiveness. I was building up this exact kind of match since I wanted to try something different. I mentioned before the 5 minutes in the ring match I did with Madman Pondo and Ian Rotten but going into further detail here can shed some light on some great booking. Having been trained as a professional wrestler I was able to hang with a face in the ring for five minutes and yet I still understood that doing a lot of complex moves or big moves would not go over well with the crowd. As far as they were concerned, I was a relatively small manager and the face was a big, strong, tough individual so it really wouldn't take much for him to beat me to a point where I couldn't even stand up. I got with the face wrestler to go over how we would play out the five minutes in a sort of broad stroke method. He wasn't a particularly good wrestler but I wanted to make sure he understood that he needed to keep the big holds to a minimum, give me plenty of time to sell things, and most importantly to execute the finale properly. The match setting up to the face having five minutes with me included a 6-foot-tall cactus which was placed into a ring corner and then the face reversed a whip out of the corner from my heel wrestler sending the heel wrestler back first into the cactus. The idea was for the grand finale to have the face wrestler to give me a full whip from the opposite side of the ring slamming into the cactus in the corner telegraphing it to the crowd and giving a nice symmetry of such a horrible move happening to both myself and my heel wrestler. Other than that, I told him I would call it in the ring with a related note about how the crowd was going to be and I wanted to make sure that this guy understood how little really needed to be done (remember, he was not a good wrestler). The unpredictable nature of professional wrestling reared its ugly head almost immediately as during the setup match after my heel wrestler had been whipped into the cactus it fell out of the corner and was now lying in the ring. So much for the grand finale, we had planned as nothing looks dumber than someone picking up a prop for a failed or repeated spot but I was able to salvage it nonetheless. As soon as the face won the match and was selling the difficulty of the victory, I grabbed the microphone and boasted to everyone that the joke was on him, I was a well-trained collegiate and professional wrestler and that he didn't have five minutes in the ring with me, I had five minutes in the ring with him. It was a typical heel arrogance but created just enough doubt in the mind of the audience that perhaps I did know a thing or two about wrestling or make them laugh at the absurdity of it. I told them to ring the bell and got into the ring where the face wrestler was propping himself up by the ring ropes. I grabbed him by the wrist to whip him across the ring and told him to reverse it with a clothesline. He came off the ropes and instead of executing a clothesline, he slipped around my side to my back and executed a belly-to-back suplex (poorly I might add) whereby I was only saved by my instinctual training and tucking my chin well beyond what I needed to as he almost put me down square on my neck. The face wrestler was not used to being in the ring with someone as lightweight as I (relatively speaking of course) so he decided to do some moves he always wanted to do. He immediately grabbed me and I immediately told him to punch me then back off and let me sell the move which he did. After the sell, he proceeded to pick me up and without any kind of warning or indication made a move to lift me off the ground so I gave him a good jump and found myself positioned above him where he then maneuvered me into a position to do Razor Ramon's "knife's edge" move. For those unfamiliar with that move, the face had his arms up above his head in sort of a Superman pose with his hands under my armpits and me facing up to the ceiling. The face then leaned forward again bringing my full weight down nearly on my neck but fortunately distributed across my shoulders. He came over to pick me up and I told him that was enough of the big moves and he needed to give me time to sell - in fact, a lot of time - and then when I fully recovered to my feet hit me with a steel chair which I would then need a lot of time to sell. He followed my instructions except of course instead of hitting me properly with a steel chair he hit me on the side of the head almost knocking me out. It was a good opportunity and time for me to blade so the blood started flowing. I noticed out of the corner of my eye that he was taunting the crowd with a second chair shot. This is not what I wanted but I had to go with it so I sold for a while finally standing up and taking the second chair shot which he executed as equally as poor as the first one. I called out for him to come over which he did and I then instructed him that we needed to slow things down and go to the mat. To his credit, he found someone in the crowd who had a flag on a pole that was about 4 feet long and he proceeded to take that stick and with me crawling across the ring rammed it into my rear end holding it and twisting it back and forth. I sold it like crazy despite the fact of wearing leather pants and not feeling anything at all. With my sense of timing, I knew we had less than a minute left at this point so when he came over, I instructed him to lock me up in a rest hold where we could talk. Once again to his credit, he tied me up like a pretzel so no one could see us talk and I explained to him that we would have to change the ending and I wanted him to when the time was right, break this rest hold, pull my shirt off then signal to the crowd and set me up for power bomb dropping me back first shirtless on to the cactus lying in the ring. He said he understood that after some more selling he broke the hold a little bit too early and started to set up for the finish. Thankfully I hired a really good staff so without prompting the ring announcer started a 10-second countdown for the crowd over the PA system. This let me perfectly know just how early the face started the sequence so I spun free from him after he removed my shirt and did a slow march directly away from him such that by the time he caught me and pulled me back into the position we were at the three count so a slight jump and hold in position at the one count over the PA then saw me smashing down on the cactus at the zero for a perfect ending. Interesting side note that has nothing to do with anything really but people always ask me about that spot and I always tell them that powerbomb onto the cactus did not hurt in the least bit as it was bumped properly and the adrenaline was flowing. If you watch the tape closely you will see me rolling around selling the agony but then I rolled a little too close and my elbow brushes lightly against one of the needles of the cactus and you see me quickly jerk it away as that hurt like hell. As a final note and word of warning for anyone planning on working with cactus, for about a week after I had a red stripe down my back from the low-level poison contained in the needles that of course, I was unaware of since I failed to properly research cactus prior to involving it in a match – a BIG violation of my own rules and I paid the price.

LADDER MATCH

The ladder match has no classic wrestling origin or comparison and for a very good reason - with possibly one or two exceptions there are no good ladder matches. The issue is very similar to the ones found with the Steel Cage match. Wrestlers find themselves balancing uncomfortably on the ladder or working around it in a very obvious way again literally destroying the willing suspension of disbelief. On the rare occasions where you have two very balanced and athletic wrestlers, they can avoid all this which results in a very satisfying daredevil/acrobatic-like match however have to ask yourself what did the ladder really add to the match? In this case, I'm not talking about a match with the belt suspended from the ceiling requiring a ladder to obtain I'm simply referring to a match that happens to have a ladder. It is in fact better option to utilize a ladder for a few high spots in an ordinary match that have highly balanced and athletic wrestlers. The daredevil aspect of it holds far greater impact when it is used sparingly as opposed to over the course of an entire match. Also, as previously stated, the focus should be on the storyline and the story of the match, not acrobatic moves.

HARDCORE WRESTLING

(you actually do need skills)

30

Hardcore wrestling is one of the most misunderstood and maligned forms of professional wrestling and with good reason. It is often said that individuals who engage in hardcore wrestling do so because they are not very good wrestlers as they are not able to do the moves, the holds and counter moves and counter holds that "traditional" wrestlers can do. I am forced to admit that in many of those cases they are correct. This however does not mean that there is no place for hardcore wrestling or that you can't be capable of doing both styles.

When engaging in hardcore wrestling the number one thing to consider, if you plan on doing it properly, is safety. Many people think that runs counter to what they have seen in hardcore matches and while they are probably correct, I would argue it's simply because they haven't seen good hardcore wrestling. I have mentioned before, one of the highlights of my career was the opportunity to manage Mad Man Pondo in his first-ever match against Abdullah The Butcher. Pondo was known for many things but one of them was a move whereby he would whip his opponent off the ropes and then using a steel stop sign blast them over the head with it. It made a great sound despite being stiff due to the nature of it being made out of steel and the sign had other uses for other spots in matches as well. Abby was aware of this move so before the match, the three of us were off in a room by ourselves going over the match when Abby asked Pondo to blast him over the head with the stop sign just as he would do in the match. Pondo and I sort of looked at each other shrugged, and then Pondo proceeded to blast Abby in the head with the stop sign. Abby stood there, thought for a moment, and then said no that was a little too much and we were going to do it differently during the match. Instead, he suggested Pondo take the edge of the stop sign and "grind" it in to the ridges in Abby's forehead which he acquired from decades of improper blading. That may seem insignificant but it points to a broader picture that safety was considered even on the simplest of moves. To illustrate further, we decided the basic plan to start with would be me grabbing Abby's leg as he was entering the ring (with one leg already in the ring) preventing him from fully entering the ring and allowing Pondo to attack him while he was fundamentally immobile. Abby would eventually get in the ring and take over dumping Pondo to the outside then I would then jump on Abby's back, he would then give me his signature forking in my forehead which would allow me to blade and then be effectively eliminated from the match so it could be just Pondo and Abby as the focus. Trust me, I was happy just getting to get forked by Abdullah the Butcher! Everything went according to plan but later in the match, Abby had Pondo by the hair and dragged him over to me while I was selling outside the ring, grabbed me by the hair, and then smashed our heads together. I sold it as a semi-knockout move and hit the guardrail and then the floor whereas Pondo being the larger wrestler smartly propped himself up against the guardrail with a less sell. Seeing me lying prone on the ground Abby walked over, motioned to the crowd, then placed his foot expertly across my chest and stood on it showing the audience that all 300+ pounds of him was standing squarely on my chest. Safety again was paramount since speaking with Abby after the match, he revealed that he had consulted decades ago with a doctor and knew the exact place to step where his weight could be distributed and no injury would result.

 A lot of hardcore wrestlers are under the delusion that in order to impress the crowd they must come up with something that has a high chance of injury themselves. It is not enough to merely get smashed over the head with an electric light tube instead they feel like they have to build a small house with the tubes in a crisscross fashion and then be thrown through them. While this might look great for a single move, I've often seen this occur relatively early in a match and now the wrestlers have to face the joy of wrestling in a ring filled with small shards of glass all over it opening up the possibility of not only cuts all over the body but eye or ear injuries that could be far more troublesome. Instead, what I recommend hardcore wrestlers focused on is presenting something the fans have either not seen before or that gives the appearance that things are out of control. There are two spots in that Abdullah the Butcher match I was directly involved in that illustrates this point. At the time we had a nice entrance that consisted of an upside-down "U" shaped truss with curtains across the top of the upside-down "U". At one point in the match, Abby grabbed me by the hair and threw me towards that entrance I suppose expecting me to hit the truss and then sell it which is what the audience was expecting as well. I of course did that but also, since I knew how the truss was assembled, positioned myself such that I loosened what I needed to in order to have the truss start to fall forward. Security was quick to catch it but it was completely unexpected and the crowd went crazy as it appeared Abby threw me hard enough into the entrance way to knock it over. Another incident to illustrate this point was that the match ended in a double count-out and the three of us went back to the locker room. Abby motioned for Pondo and me to come over to him next to a second door and he asked me where this led. I told him it went back out to the arena but behind the audience near the merchandise tables. He said perfect but when we motioned to start to go out he stopped us and simply said "wait for it". He then listened to the crowd who was cheering "more! more! more!" and yet he did not make a move until just as the crowd chant was starting to die down. We then burst through the door with Abby attacking Pondo finally knocking him to the ground near the end of the merchandise tables. Abby then set his sights on me grabbing me and throwing me towards a merchandise table. The expected response was for me to slam my head against the table and then sell it as I flopped back to the ground. Going after the unexpected I threw myself across the top of the table and used my left hand to grab the lip of the table which caused it to completely flip over sending the merchandise flying and landing on me, completely covering me. As this was so unexpected the crowd completely lost their shit. These are just small examples but hopefully, it gets across a larger point - hardcore wrestling is not as much about how deep or badly cut someone is but about how unpredictable your actions can be.

There is another aspect of hardcore wrestling that I feel needs to be touched on. When getting in to hardcore wrestling I remember Mad Man Pondo had a list of "common sense" rules for things he would not do. His list was in fact very "common sense" based and I applauded him for it. He basically said he would not be involved in a match that involved fire, involved animals, or required him to perform barefoot. The logic was sound as fire and animals are completely unpredictable no matter what anyone thinks or what safeguards are put into place. If you have any doubts reference my previous story with the fire at the frat house where I took every precaution but the other wrestler did not and the result was almost burning down a frat house. The barefoot stipulation had more to do with health and pain tolerance than anything else. The bottom of the feet are rather thin-skinned and walking around in glass or thumbtacks is going to hurt like hell plus, and far more importantly, if you injure the feet and have difficulty walking you can't effectively wrestle in the ring, therefore, you can't make money. The problem however is that being involved in hardcore matches lends itself to a diminishing return on investment. That is to say that once you use one light tube in a match you can't just keep using one light tube. In order to give the audience something new the thought that most wrestlers have is just – "more". Two light tubes then four, then 12, etc., etc. The end result of such an escalation is after many years of hardcore wrestling all over including in Japan and other countries Mad Man Pondo had broken every one of his "common sense" rules but had not suffered any permanent or career-ending injuries because of it. Speaking to him about this after the fact he revealed that it was nothing more than luck that spared him serious injury in all those circumstances where he performed with fire, with animals, or barefoot. Considering real options for permanent life-altering injury or even death you must strive to remove luck entirely from the wrestling ring. That is why I say you must follow the three rules and when engaging in hardcore wrestling you make every effort to mitigate the chance of serious injury such as we did when watering down ourselves prior to the exploding barbed wire death match or not caving in and actually standing firm on the no fire, no animal and no barefoot rules.

One final thing regarding hardcore wrestling that I would really like to drive home. The greatest hardcore wrestlers of all time will tell you that hardcore moves are best utilized as an exclamation point throughout the story as opposed to the story alone. If you start your match out smashing someone over the head with some object causing them to bleed and the rest of the match is just cutting each other for more blood you have effectively desensitized the audience to the very actions you are engaging in. This once again leads to an escalation of risk which can turn into an escalation in the chance of injury - permanent or otherwise. The better option is to tell compelling stories in the match and utilize the hardcore to really drive home the danger, the viciousness, or the hatred involved in the story. What I often get in the way of pushback for this is a wrestler will say "well, the crowd is used to seeing nothing but hardcore now so that's what we have to give them since they would be bored with your normal match that only had small amounts of hardcore in". This could not be further from the truth since while there may be a small percentage of the audience that is there to see nothing more than the train wreck the other 95% of the audience find it far more interesting if they know the detailed story of why there is a train wreck.

BACKYARD / MODERN WRESTLING

(learn to slow down)

32

What I have found over the years is that both backyard wrestlers, and most modern wrestlers, do everything at a very fast pace. From interviews to ring entrances to moves and transitions are all done at an accelerated pace that does nothing more than diminish the impact of all those things.

First, to clarify, the term backyard wrestler was more of a saying in the 1990s but it describes an ongoing situation. Anyone who is not professionally trained yet engages in professional wrestling activity either merely in their backyard (or basement) for themselves or even before a hand full of friends can be described as a backyard wrestler. The essential component is that they are not trained. My references to the modern wrestlers are based on when this book was written was in the year 2022. Reading this book 10,25 or 100 years later "modern" wrestlers may act differently. It is my hope that they do act differently in a positive way by adopting the concepts in this book. Either way understanding the time reference is one thing but it cannot be used to dismiss the valuable lesson that can be learned here – IE: "That was written 20 years ago so it no longer applies".

There are quite a few issues with doing everything sped up and I mentioned the biggest one at the beginning of this section - the loss of impact. If you body slam someone then immediately picked them up and do another move and then immediately picked them up and do another move etc. etc. without giving your opponent time to sell the move to the audience then the move holds no credibility. Why would you do a move if it doesn't really affect anybody and you just have to do more and more moves to achieve the same end result? Wrestling moves and holds are supposed to hurt the opponent wearing them down to a point where they are unable to raise their shoulder for a three count. If moves and holds are not given sufficient time to be sold then it breaks the willing suspension of disbelief and the pinfall becomes unrealistic and lacks credibility. People need time to process what they are witnessing. They need more than just big moves to become emotionally invested. Bringing back the comparison to the movies, there is a reason you don't see a 1 hour 45 minute movie of nothing but big, unconnected action sequences. A well-structured movie, just like a well-structured wrestling storyline, will take time building up characters and motivation sprinkling in a fair amount of action sequences but building up to a big huge action sequence involving the characters at the end. Swap out action sequence with match mechanics and you have a great blueprint for a storyline that can then translate in to a match.

Another issue with speeding everything up is it comes off as insecure to the audience. Think of the insecure guy hitting on a girl that is stuttering, stammering, and quickly blurting out sentences or the fast-talking car salesman listing feature after feature of the car without listening to you. Both scenarios come off as completely insecure as those activities are rightfully seen as a mask for the lack of confidence. Executing a big move on the wrestler and then acknowledging the crowd, seeking their approval, or rubbing it in their face shows you are confident that your move was powerful enough to do some damage to your opponent and the audience picks up on that. It is the primary reason that when a heel executes a big move on the face and then turns to play to the crowd and the face no sells the move the fans go crazy even more because they wish to see the heel humiliated and the heel is so confident that their move was so awesome but the audience knows that it wasn't and that their hero, the face, is about to get one up on the heel. Quickly rushing through the above-listed scenario results in zero interest and zero impact from the crowd.

CONCLUSION

(where do we go from here)

34

My career was long, fruitful, and ended by my own decision to move on. I say this for no other reason than to make it clear I am only able to make that statement because I followed my own advice in this book. Yes, mistakes were made, with the exception of the torn ACL only minor injuries were racked up but at the end of the day I made money, still have my health and faculties, and have several lifetimes of stories and experiences that so few other people will ever have. If I had not applied the three rules if I did not understand psychology and most importantly if I didn't have the ability to be honest with myself and all the people that worked for me, I would have none of those things.

The answer to the question of where to go from here is simple and obvious. If you're willing to use this book as is designed for reference, structure, and possibly even inspiration combined with the determination and willingness to work hard then the only place to go is to better and better wrestling experiences. I used the word experiences specifically since this book is not merely limited in how to have a better match or how to tell a better story or how to engage a crowd more. It obviously touches on all those things and I sincerely hope that after reading everything here you begin to understand the big picture and how it is all connected and how it could all be utilized to create something truly memorable and truly impactful. If you want to strip it all down to its barest idea everything in this book is designed to help wrestlers connect emotionally with the crowd.

I'll share one final humorous anecdote to illustrate how powerful this can be. I was running a monthly show not too far from where I lived and in fact, I was doing a great job getting over as a completely vicious and psychologically unhinged heel manager willing to do anything and say anything to win and to encourage my wrestlers to hurt and humiliate their opponents. Believe it or not, it's part of the story and not ego when I say I also happened to have at that time a very attractive girlfriend who was living with me. There was a Walgreens not too far from my home that she and I would frequently patronize and we were actually there enough to know the people that worked there. When I say "know the people who work there" I don't mean that we knew them personally or even engaged in any sort of conversation, we simply were able to say "the teen guy" or the "rude pharmacy lady" and we knew who the other was talking about. One day my girlfriend went to Walgreens by herself (1st time if I am not mistaken) and when she came back, she actually looked angry and said "you are not going to believe what just happened to me". Curious I asked what happened and she related the following story. She said that when she entered the Walgreens, she immediately noticed the teen guy was at the checkout. As I said we'd been there enough for me to know that she was talking about the probably 16 or 17-year-old guy that was probably pretty popular as he was a decent-looking fellow, seemed nice but he never said anything more than what our total bill was. She continued with her story saying that for whatever reason this time, from the moment she stepped foot in the store, he looked very nervous and seemed fixated on her. She grabbed what she needed and proceeded to wait in line at the checkout as there were a couple of people ahead of her. He said she noticed the young guy taking many opportunities for sideways glances at her and she had a pretty good idea of what she thought was coming. It was finally her turn and there was no one behind her so she said the kid nervously checked her out and after handing her the receipt very nervously, stammered in his speech and asked if he could ask her a question. This was nothing new for her and she had her "let him down gently" speech all ready to go since she was regularly asked out on dates by random guys. He finally mustered up the courage and said "Are you Shriek's girlfriend?" She

| 201 |

said to me she was completely shocked and appalled and she genuinely thought he was going to ask her out and was more than a little hurt that he was more interested in finding out if she was my girlfriend than in trying to hit on her. She did recover and said, "Yes I am". His reply was priceless as he said "I don't know how you do it, that guy is crazy". I'll fully admit to possibly sliding into character a little bit every time after that when I went back to the Walgreens and saw him but the real point here is that such a connection was made that despite seeing me in "real life" he was convinced enough and engaged enough to think that the character and their actions were "real" to him.

David "Shriek" Chapman

Since I'll never know when anyone is reading this book, I can't know what will be on it but please check out my website (or whatever exists when you read this book) at:

https://artandscienceofwrestling.com

Go Forth

And use the tools you have learned here!

www.ingramcontent.com/pod-product-compliance
Lightning Source LLC
Chambersburg PA
CBHW051431290426
44109CB00016B/1511